Pocket Pups

THE DEFINITIVE GUIDE TO DIMINUTIVE DOGS

by Nikki Moustaki

with photographs by Christopher Appoldt

TREEHOUSE
BOOKS

Read the word. Read the world.
Build your home library, today!
1430 W. Susquehanna Ave Philadelphia, PA 19121
www.treehouse-books.org

EDITORIAL
Andrew DePrisco *Editor-in-Chief*
Peter Bauer *Managing Editor*
Amy Deputato *Senior Editor*
Jonathan Nigro *Editor*
Matt Strubel *Assistant Editor*

ART
Sherise Buhagiar *Graphic Layout*
Bill Jonas *Book Design*
Joanne Muzyka *Digital Art*

Copyright © 2007

Kennel Club Books®
A DIVISION OF BOWTIE, INC.
40 Broad Street, Freehold, NJ 07728 USA

Additional photographs by: Bernd Brinkmann, Chelle Calbert, Jerome Cushman, Tara Darling, Isabelle Français, Leah Getty, Wolfgang Knorr, Al Linn, Therese Murphy, Stewart Event Images and ZUMA Press.

Library of Congress Cataloging-in-Publication Data

Moustaki, Nikki, 1970-
  Pocket pups / by Nikki Moustaki.
    p. cm.
  Includes index.
  ISBN-13: 978-1-59378-676-2
  ISBN-10: 1-59378-676-X
  1. Toy dogs. I. Title.
  SF429.T7M68 2007
  636.76--dc22

                                        2007004810

Printed and bound in Singapore

10 9 8 7 6 5 4 3 2 1

Contents

A Pooch in My Pocketbook

Pomeranian in a pink Prada purse...a Havanese in a hand-crafted Hermés handbag...a Chinese Crested in chic Chanel...the dog world's gone to hell in a very expensive handbag!

Toy dogs, teacup pups, purebred pooches and minuscule mutts of questionable pedigree—it doesn't matter what they're called, as long as they look fabulous in a sweater and can fit beneath one arm. Today, the scope of the toy-dog phenomenon ranges much wider than Paris Hilton's high-profile Chihuahua or Britney Spears's million-dollar furbaby. Nowadays, every designer shoulder bag on the boulevard contains a furry face, a trendy tail and a bejeweled collar.

Once again, the toy dog has become a fashion accessory. It's no surprise, really, since toy dogs came into being for the sole purpose of decorating their mistresses' laps and baskets. The toy dog is timeless, and a classic never goes out of style. When your Jimmy Choo pumps have become passé (never!), you can toss them in the Salvation Army donation pile. Some lucky lady will look fabulous in your old kicks! But lucky for you, you'll never have to worry about your Papillon, Havanese, Chinese Crested or Silky Terrier going out of style, so don't even think of giving him up for a fast-talking gecko or a night-crawling kinkajou. A dog of any size requires a dedicated guardian who is willing to offer care for the entire life of the little wagger; in the case of small dogs, that can add up to much more than a decade's worth of commitment.

Little Fidos have their own particular challenges that owners should address well before ordering diamond-studded custom collars. Just because a dog is small

doesn't mean that owning him is easy! Pocket pooches live in their own little kingdoms where they have a somewhat delusional view of life. Most have moments where they believe that they are huge dogs and will challenge other animals that could trounce them to death with one blow, like carriage horses on Fifth Avenue, Great Danes in the dog park and bitter ex-beaus. Fifteen minutes after he has one of his "big-dog" moments, Tiny will sidle up to you, tail between his legs, ears slicked back, eyes glassy and wide, with a look that can only mean, "Can you *pweeze* pick me up because I am just a *wittle* doggie. And while you're at it, can you *pweeze* get me a smidgen of caviar? The good stuff, not that cheap stuff you tried to pawn off on me the last time I attempted to attack the neighbor's Rottweiler through the fence."

SMALL DOG CRITERIA

For this book, we consider dogs under 14 inches tall (at the shoulder) and under 20 pounds to qualify as pocket pooches. Ideally, a small dog should be able to ride comfortably in a fashionable bag or go unnoticed through the front door of Saks wrapped in your cashmere pashmina. Some pocket-sized dogs, like small Beagles, fit the size parameters and would look cute in a sweater. However, the once common pocket Beagles, small enough to fit into a horseman's saddle bag, aren't commonly bred these days, and the snazzy 13-inch model would not tolerate being clutched and suffocated in a Persian wrap.

Don't be fooled by a breed's name and reputation when it comes to size, because some of the pocket-pooch breeds can come in medium-sized packages rather than extra-small. For example, even though a Miniature Schnauzer can still be classified as a pocket pooch based on the aforementioned criteria, it's also possible to find Miniature Schnauzers out there who weigh 30 pounds or more.

TEACUPS

Teacup dogs are the teensy versions of the toy breeds. The smallest of these dogs will stay under 3 pounds as full-grown adults and can set your bank account back anywhere from $1,500 to $13,000.

A steamy controversy has been brewing about teacup dogs. Some people believe that they have too many congenital health disorders to justify breeding them. Other people feel that quality breeders are working on the health issues through selective breeding and are creating better, hardier teacups. If you want a teacup that's going to remain small, request that the breeder hang on to the pup for a few months to make sure that Speck isn't going to turn into Jumbo (albeit relatively speaking).

Further, Tiny can easily turn into Tubby if you feed him too many toast triangles from the table or carry him constantly instead of letting him frisk at your side from time to time.

"Teacup" is really just a marketing term for dogs that are bred to be much smaller than the show standard. Just as humans vary in height and weight, so do dogs. For example, the preferred weight for a show Maltese is between 4 and 6 pounds, yet many pet Maltese average between 8 and 10 pounds and a "teacup" Maltese may weigh only 3 pounds. They are all Maltese, but the smaller dog has been "bred down" using selective breeding.

To breed teacup pups, breeders keep the smallest pup in a litter (formerly known as the "runt" of the litter) and breed it with another "runt" or small dog of the same breed. The resulting puppies most likely will be small. Perhaps there will be an even smaller runt in that litter, which is then bred to another small dog. Sometimes breeders will inbreed (e.g., sibling to sibling or offspring to parent) to create even smaller dogs, but

this can create serious health and temperament problems.

Be very cautious when you buy a miniature version of any dog. These little dogs are fragile and can be injured easily. A minor illness in a larger dog can be fatal to a teacup, as tiny dogs dehydrate quickly. They can also have bone

and liver issues, as well as low blood sugar. Fortunately, veterinarians are getting savvier about treating teensy dogs; this includes having things like small needles and mini-sized pills on hand. If you have a teacup, make sure that your veterinarian knows how to properly treat him.

YOUR POOCH IN PUBLIC

Having a small dog can be a lot of fun and is a great icebreaker at cocktail parties, especially when Bijou pokes his head out of your Hermés bag, but the attention that these little pooches get from strangers can turn even the sweetest little doggie into a

colossal monster. Small dogs are subject to being grabbed and poked and scooped up and smooched—and many people don't think to ask first. This can create a fearful and nervous little dog that might resort to growling and biting to defend himself against a perceived threat. When you put the pooch in a cute coat, he's doubly apt to get pawed by an ill-mannered stranger. This is why pocket pooches need to be heavily socialized—you and your tiny dog are much more likely to be approached than someone with a Rottweiler or Bullmastiff.

SPOILED ROTTEN

Little dogs often get a bad rap for poor behavior. They are sneered at for being nervous, yappy and aggressive. But this isn't because they are small. It's because they are often spoiled and untrained. Anyone with a 100-pound dog (or even a 30-pound dog) knows that training is essential. If you've ever had a Great Dane poop on your rug or a German Shepherd bare his teeth at you, you'd know to fly past *go* and get your dog to a trainer ASAP. But people with nippy, nasty little dogs often forgo training for the old standby— picking up Poochie, baby-talking him and toting him off to his next victim. Dogs that are snatched up and whisked away from everyday situations never learn how to be a part of the human or canine world. They become the canine equivalent of "antisocial." Often, the only thing that little dogs learn is how to be carried around and growl at strangers. No wonder some people believe that these pooches aren't worth the trouble of punting them through a set of goalposts. It's the owner's obligation to teach the dog the basics of living among humans.

consider a medium-sized breed or at least one of the larger pocket pooches (unless, of course, your nanny, chauffeur and full-time masseur can keep an eye on the interaction between your kids and the pup!).

GETTING GLAM

One of the most amusing aspects of having a pocket pooch is shopping! Canine couture comes in the tiniest sizes, and the shops have trouble keeping the smallest sizes in stock. Little dogs look great in shiny collars and fancy coats. Remember, it's all about the accessories! On the other hand, can you imagine putting a rhinestone collar on a Labrador? It doesn't have quite the same effect.

TOTS AND TEENIES

Kids and dogs are like crackers and Brie—one wouldn't be as good without the other. But kids are a serious hazard to dogs under 15 pounds, especially kids younger than about eight or so, depending on their maturity level. A teacup pup doesn't stand a chance in a household with a toddler. If you have young children,

FUN WITH FIDO

Because you can take your pocket pooch just about anywhere unnoticed (unless he insists on monopolizing your conversations—Chihuahuas are to be seen and not heard), you can have a lot of fun with your dog simply by toting him around on your errands, taking him to the movies or enjoying a dinner at an outdoor café. You can take your dog on family vacations where he really will be considered part of the family—hotels now offer packages that include doggie beds, healthy room-service menu choices, dog walking and spa treatments like massage and doggie pedicures.

If you live in an urban area, you might find a local "Yappy Hour" at a doggie daycare or upscale hotel, and even singles' events for dog lovers. Some daycare centers offer small-dog play nights where dogs under 20 pounds can romp without fear of being mauled by a 100-pounder. Some urban dog runs even have sections reserved for small dogs.

SHOWING

Most people don't show their dogs in conformation events, but if you develop a passion for your breed you may want to check out dog shows to see what they're all about. Conformation events are sanctioned by clubs, like the American Kennel Club or the United Kennel Club, that are dedicated to the preservation of purebred dogs. In order for your dog to participate in these events, he or she has to be intact (not neutered or spayed), has to be registered with the sponsoring kennel club, has to be at least six months old (for AKC and UKC), has to have a pedigree and must not have any disqualifying faults. Showing is not for the average person: you have to be willing to invest a lot of time, effort and money in order to raise and train good-quality dogs and travel to the shows. It takes a very special and dedicated person to participate successfully in dog showing. It's a ball to attend shows as a spectator, though (but leave Binky at home).

SPORTS AND ACTIVITIES

It's much easier to get involved in other types of organized canine sports and activities than it is to get involved in conformation showing, though you won't spend any less effort or time doing it. Events like obedience trials, agility trials, flyball and canine freestyle (dancing with dogs) take quite a lot of dedication in training, but even the novice can get in on the fun and learn a lot. As you work with your dog and progress to higher levels of competition, your knowledge and expertise will increase, too.

Some pocket dogs excel in competitive events like these; Dachshunds and the small terriers can even compete in earthdog events if owners don't mind their dogs' getting down and dirty in traditional terrier fashion. Other small dogs can't be bothered with such things, and many toy dogs are happy to simply excel at napping. Quite honestly, the sport that the really teeny dogs are good at is a sale at Saks.

PARIS HILTON

Paris and Tinkerbell

at the 2005 Gay Pride Parade in West Hollywood

Star Dogs

Celebs love tiny dogs! From Paris Hilton to Hilary Duff to Star Jones Reynolds, a lot of the A-listers have gotten in on the trend. This can make small dogs seem like a fad or an accessory, but they are neither. Many of the small dogs were developed to be companions and have served faithfully in this capacity for hundreds of years. The Pekingese, for example, was a prized royal companion in China as far back as 2000 BC. There's nothing new or trendy about honoring and spoiling a little dog. In fact, stealing a Pekingese in China in ancient times was punishable by death.

Little dogs make perfect sense for celebrities who are always on the go. It's easy to pack a Chihuahua into a bag for a day on the movie set or lunch at Spago. Little dogs are adaptable, easy to hide and just as personable as dogs 50 times their size. So it's not surprising that the average mortal (that's you and me) has fallen for those furry faces, too. Just because you have a hectic life and can't rush home to walk a Golden Retriever doesn't mean that you should be devoid of doggie love. Little dogs have nothing to do with fashion, and they aren't nice just because you can put them in bag that matches your shoes. They are filled with a weighty Shakespearean love that only a dog and star-crossed lovers can offer.

TORI SPELLING

TORI AND HER LITTLE ORPHAN PUG

AT THE BOW WOW WEEN DOGGIE COSTUME CONTEST

REBECCA GAYHEART

Rebecca and her portable pup
at *The Royal Tenenbaums* premiere

JESSICA SIMPSON

MALTIPOO DAISY AND JESSICA
ON *LATE NIGHT WITH DAVID LETTERMAN*

CHRISTINA AGUILERA

Christina brought a friend

to help her open Harrod's summer sale

HAYLIE DUFF

Haylie and her Pom

at the Febreze Fresh pet fashion show

PAM AND HER CHIHUAHUA

OUT AND ABOUT IN MALIBU

PAMELA ANDERSON

STAR JONES REYNOLDS

STAR AND PINKY

AT NYC's SELF CENTER OPENING

BRITNEY SPEARS

BRITNEY OUTFITS CHIHUAHUA

BIT BIT IN STYLE

CARMEN ELECTRA

Carmen gets a pocket-pooch smooch during Olympus Fashion Week in NYC

DAVEIGH CHASE

Daveigh's pup travels first-class at the Night of 100 Stars gala

PAULA ABDUL

Paula and her brood
at the Paws for Style fashion show

FRAN DRESCHER

FRAN AND POM ESTHER

AT THE WB NETWORK'S PRESS TOUR PARTY

Enter the Pooches

If pocket pooches have to be able to be carried in a bag and look spectacular in a sweater, then there are a lot of breeds to choose from. This chapter outlines the characteristics of the small breeds and will give you an idea of which is best for you and your family.

Each breed's group classification is listed according to the American Kennel Club's (AKC) registry unless otherwise noted. Heights and weights are based on AKC breed standards when those measurements are given in the standards. If the breed is not recognized by the AKC, heights and weights are based on the registering organization's standard. Height typically refers to the dog's height at the shoulder, and upper height and weight limits are included even if they fall outside our pocket-pup parameters. Remember that breed standards list ideal criteria for show specimens, so pet dogs may not conform exactly to the guidelines listed. Further, teacup varieties are not included in breed standards, so these tiny dogs will be smaller than the measurements given. The clothing, food and activities listed under "preferences" were voted on by the dogs themselves and thus are not necessarily condoned or recommended by the author.

Affenpinscher

Let's Monkey Around

"Mustached, fun-loving toy dog seeks sassy lady to escort him to hot city spots."

Group: Toy

Breed Club URL:
www.affenpinscher.org

Details:

Height: 9½ to 11½ inches

Weight: 7 to 9 pounds

Coat: Dense and wiry

Grooming Face groomed to accentuate the monkey-like appearance; coat neat but shaggy

Health: Skin and flea allergies

Lifespan: 12 to 15 years

Profile:

The name of this German breed literally translates to "monkey-like terrier," and the French have termed him the "mustached devil." Whatever you call him, the Affenpinscher is courageous, tenacious, intelligent and sensitive, bred as a ratter like his ancestor, the Miniature Schnauzer. The breed has been known since the 17th century, but came to the US in 1935. Breeding stopped during and after World War II and did not resume until 1949, when fanciers sought to revive the bloodlines. A little dog with a Napoleon complex isn't unusual, and the Affenpinscher certainly follows suit, willing to take on dogs ten times his size. This breed is all attitude but also excels in training and will do anything for a laugh, though house-training is often a challenge. He requires a creative and patient trainer who knows that this thinking dog gets bored with endless repetition. Protective to a fault, he makes a great watchdog, but the Affen's human pack leaders need to enforce that he's not the ruler of the roost, as he's likely to want to take over. When he understands where he ranks in the pack, he is affectionate and loyal.

Preferences:

Best Couture: Bumble-bee striped sweater and matching booties

Favorite Foods: Banana chips, anything ending in "-wurst"

Activities: Dancing, boxing, circus tricks

American Eskimo Dog

Ice, Ice, Baby!

"When it's cold outside, the Eskie can heat things up!"

Group: Non-Sporting

Breed Club URL: www.edca.org

Details:

Height:	*Toy:* 9 to and including 12 inches; *Miniature:* over 12 to and including 15 inches
Weight:	*Toy:* up to 10 pounds; *Mini:* 10 to 20 pounds
Coat:	Dense double coat of snow white
Grooming:	Weekly brushing; absolutely no trimming; heavy shed twice a year
Tail:	Profusely coated, carried loosely over back
Health:	Patellar luxation; progressive retinal atrophy; elbow dysplasia
Lifespan:	12 to 16 years

Profile:

An American fairy tale: a miniature snow-white dog in a big coat accompanied German, Dutch and Italian immigrants to American shores. The American Eskimo Dog is a direct descendant of European spitz dogs, such as the Pomeranian, Keeshond and German Spitz. A lesser known Italian dog, the Volpino Italiano, is a similar breed to the American Eskimo, though it is rare indeed. The Toy and the Miniature Eskies fit pocket-pooch criteria. The AKC also recognizes a Standard variety, but you'd need a Louis Vuitton steamer trunk to haul him around.

An eager-to-please companion dog, the American Eskimo makes a smart and friendly family dog, though he's a bit reserved with the "extended family." He learns quickly but tires of repetition. Keep him busy and involved in your daily routine. Discourage barking from a young age or you'll have to move to 99500 so as not to bother your neighbors—yes, that's Anchorage, AK.

Preferences:

Best Couture:	Loose-knit poncho and beret
Favorite Foods:	Goose pate, pork bellies
Activities:	Chasing ice cubes, digging, chillin'

American Hairless Terrier

Naked Lunch & Dinner

"Meal companion wanted—nudist preferred"

Group: Terrier (United Kennel Club)

Breed Club URL: www.ahta.info

Details:

Height: 10 to 18 inches

Weight: Approx. 7 to 17 pounds

Coat: None! Does have dander and sweats when hot or scared

Grooming: Lotion for dry skin (no lanolin); sunscreen for warm months; attendance to any scratches or cuts; nail trimming

Tail: Full length

Health: Pimples; skin allergies; rashes; sunburn if not protected

Lifespan: 14 to 16 years

Profile:

If you like the Rat Terrier, you'll love the American Hairless. He's got all the goodies of a tenacious terrier and none of the shedding. In the early 1970s a mutation of the Rat Terrier appeared in a litter—a hairless dog. This female was bred to a coated dog and eventually produced two hairless offspring—the entire foundation of the breed was born of these three dogs. Fortunately, this breed has none of the congenital problems that the other hairless breeds have. As a companion, this breed is affectionate, feisty and fearless, tending toward stubbornness in training unless the trainer is creative and takes measures to not bore the dog. They are not yappy in general, but they will noisily guard their property. More good news is that they don't get fleas, and most people that are allergic to dogs show no allergy symptoms to the American Hairless. The bad news is that you can't tie any cute bows on top of their heads!

Preferences:

Best Couture: Body suit in summer; sweater and winter coat

Favorite Foods: Yogurt, peanut butter, squirrel pie

Activities: Strip poker, swimming, day spas

Australian Terrier

Let's Hang 20!

"Come Down Under for a swim you'll dig."

Group: Terrier

Breed Club URL: www.australianterrier.org

Preferences:

Best Couture:	"Stud" or "Princess" t-shirt
Favorite Foods:	Gator burgers, lamb chops
Activities:	Digging on the beach, evacuating mud puddles

Details:

Height:	10 to 11 inches
Weight:	9 to 14 pounds
Coat:	Soft undercoat; rough longer outer coat
Grooming:	Weekly brushing; trimming around face and feet; bathing when needed, but not often; hand stripping for appropriate coat texture, if desired.
Tail:	Docked
Health:	No congenital problems of note; diabetes; joint problems; flea allergies.
Lifespan:	15 to 16 years

Profile:

Originally bred to kill rodents and snakes, the Australian Terrier is courageous, bold and easily trained. He is born with a wide streak of "aim to please" and makes a great watchdog. He is good with respectful children and is just as happy with a life on the farm as he is in a townhouse strewn with a lot of toys. Related to the ever-popular Yorkie, the Aussie goes back even further, and he's bigger, tougher and feistier. Though he's a plucky little dog, as he'd need to be to bite off a snake's head, he does fairly well tucked away in a designer bag (as long as it's not snakeskin!) and is not the typical spoiled doggie you'd see at a Sunday sidewalk brunch.

Bichon Frise

Angel Has Halo to Share

"Perfect French lady seeks guardian angel or wealthy patron saint."

Group: Non-Sporting

Breed Club URL: www.bichon.org

Profile:

More than a Poodle with extra fluff and pizzazz, the Bichon is one of the oldest breeds, having been depicted in art as long as 2,000 years ago, and was brought to Europe in the 1300s from the Mediterranean. The French adopted this dog in the 1400s, and it soared in popularity. He was the most pampered and perfumed dog around, the companion of royals and the very wealthy. By the late 1800s he went out of fashion and began to become one of the many breeds found scraping up a living on the street. American soldiers brought the Bichon back to the US after World War II, and he immediately gained fans that revived the breed into a favored salon dog once again. He is a sturdy, amiable and adaptable companion, a true "people dog" that loves to be with his favorite person as much as possible.

Details:

Height:	9 to 12 inches
Weight:	7 to 12 pounds
Coat:	Soft, curly undercoat and denser, coarser outer coat; does not shed
Grooming:	Professional grooming needed to maintain full coat in typical style; can be clipped down in pet trim
Tail:	Natural, curled over the back
Health:	Skin allergies; dental problems; joint problems; eye and ear problems
Lifespan:	14 to 15 years

Preferences:

Best Couture:	Anything silk with tassels and beads
Favorite Foods:	Cottage cheese, fruit roll-ups, pop tarts
Activities:	Seaweed wraps, dog shows, birthday parties

Bolognese

La Bella Vita, Baby

"Saucy Mediterranean searching for meaty romance."

Group: Companion Dog
(United Kennel Club)

Breed Club URL:
http://members.aol.com/
BologneseAmerica/bca.htm and
www.bologneseclubus.com

Details:

Height:	9 to 12 inches
Weight:	8 to 14 pounds
Coat:	Thin, fluffy, silky, fly-away coat; non-shedding
Grooming:	Brushing three days a week; bathing when necessary; professional grooming
Health:	No major health issues
Lifespan:	14 years

Profile:

This Italian breed is another "white and fluffy," a popular theme among the pocket pooches. It is also called the Bichon Bolognese, but looks more like a poodle-fied Maltese. Like many other of the "white and fluffies," the Bolognese is an ancient breed, written about in literature by Aristotle as far back as 322 BC. In the late 1500s Philip II, the King of Spain, received two Bolognese dogs and said that they were gifts befitting an emperor. As a companion, the Bolognese is loyal and docile, but may tend toward couch-potato-hood. He responds best to positive-rein-forcement training, such as clicker train-ing, and doesn't do well with a harsh hand. Spoiling and pampering suits this breed perfectly.

Preferences:

Best Couture:	Flannel jammies and a Donald Pliner leather tote
Favorite Foods:	Anything Italian, polenta, sausage, antipasto
Activities:	Wine making, catnapping

Border Terrier

Foxes, Don't Bolt Just Yet!

"Dashing little guy seeks twitchy-tailed hottie for dirty fun."

Group: Terrier

Breed Club URL:
http://clubs.akc.org/btcoa

Details:

Height:	10 to 11 inches
Weight:	11½ to 15½ pounds
Coat:	Wiry with a soft undercoat; sheds moderately
Grooming:	Weekly brushing; non-shedding treatments; hand stripping twice a year
Tail:	Natural
Health:	Luxating patella; seizures; allergies; heart defects.
Lifespan:	12 to 15 years

Profile:

Because of his scruffy appearance, the Border Terrier is often mistaken for a mutt, but he has actually been around as a vermin hunter in England since the late 1700s, perhaps even earlier. He is related to the other terriers of that region, like the Bedlington and the Dandie Dinmont. He is an easily trainable breed for the average pet home, but he isn't seen all that often in the obedience ring. He is spunky and willing to please, his alertness makes him a good watchdog and he isn't known for excessive barking. As with most other small dogs, especially the terriers, enforce strict supervision around children. These little dogs are cute, but they are quick to defend themselves and won't tolerate much ear- and fur-pulling.

Preferences:

Best Couture:	Baseball cap and Doggles®
Favorite Foods:	Pork shoulder, beef stew, ice cubes
Activities:	Fetching, chasing cats, landscaping

Boston Terrier

Give Me Liver or Give Me Death!

"Faithful and loyal All-American guy demands better than pub-quality service."

Group: Non-Sporting

Breed Club URL: www.bostonterrier
clubofamerica.org

Details:

Height: 10 to 16 inches

Weight: Up to 25 pounds

Coat: Short; sheds

Grooming: Weekly rubdown with a
                grooming mitt

Health: Gets cold and overheated
                easily; airway obstruction;
                hypothyroidism; eye
                problems

Lifespan: 10 to 14 years

Profile:

Deemed "The American Gentleman," this American-bred dog started in the mid-1800s in the Northeast as a cross between Bull Terriers and Bulldogs. His fearless nature makes him a great watch-dog, but his appearance is less than intimi-dating. He is good with well-mannered chil-dren and other pets, as long as he is raised with them. Though he has a strong and compact body, he is victim to the weather and can't stand excessive cold or heat. His intelligence makes him very trainable, though he's much more content to nap at your feet than to perform in organized sports. Three moderate walks a day are just fine for him.

Preferences:

Best Couture: Warm coats and
                      sweaters, tailored
                      formalwear and
                      top hat

Favorite Foods: New England clam
                      chowder, lobster, baked
                      beans (of course!)

Activities: Tea parties, dressing
                      up, bird and whale
                      watching

Brussels Griffon

A Gruff & Tumble Romance

"Belgian-born spiffy Griff seeks friend who likes it rough."

Group: Toy

Breed Club URL:
www.brussels-griffon.info

Details:

Height: 7 to 8 inches

Weight: 8 to 12 pounds

Coat: Occurs in both rough (long) and smooth (short) coats; short coat sheds

Grooming: Rough coat requires stripping of the body coat and scissoring around the face; smooth coat needs weekly brushing

Tail: Docked

Health: Eye injuries; subluxated patella; breathing problems

Lifespan: 12 to 14 years

Profile:

A "griffon" is a mythological animal, but in dog talk it means "wiry coat." The Affenpinscher is behind this sturdy Belgian breed; other ancestors include the English Toy Spaniel, the Pug and possibly the Yorkshire Terrier. The "Griff" originated as a ratter in the stables of Belgium, but this terrier-like dog was eventually bred with the Pug in the 19th century to create a dog with a smooth coat and a shorter snout with an undershot jaw. These dogs were then crossed with English Toy Spaniels. The breed's job as a vermin hunter faded as his role as a companion came into vogue. He's a ringer at obedience trials, being a clever and eager student. His exuberance often gets the best of him, however, and he is known to challenge much larger dogs to duels that he may lose if he doesn't retreat. He doesn't take well to being left alone for long periods and can suffer separation anxiety.

He comes in two coat types: the rough-coated variety is a wiry, scruffy fellow and the smooth-coated variety is also known as the Brabançon; both coat types can occur in the same litter. Coat colors are red, belge (reddish brown mixed with black), black and tan and solid black.

Preferences:

Best Couture: Leather bomber jacket and spiked collar

Favorite Foods: Mussels, mayonnaise, white asparagus

Activities: Open-air dining, carriage rides, eating crickets

Cairn Terrier

There's No Place Like Home

"Munchkins and Kansas mutts needn't apply...Toto wants a real man."

Group: Terrier

Breed Club URL: www.cairnterrier.org

Profile:

The Cairn Terrier is the original carry-on pooch, classically represented by Toto, the fearless moppet in the wicker basket that Dorothy carried all over the wonderful land of Oz. This hardy breed originated in England in the late 1700s and was bred as a vermin hunter. Today he's just as happy on a bustling sidewalk as he is chasing rats in the stable. No longer stuck in Kansas, the Cairn can be seen in cities and suburbs as well as on hobby farms and in other rural settings. This sturdy portable pup is great with children and does well with a firm and patient trainer.

Details:

Height:	9½ to 10 inches
Weight:	13 to 14 pounds
Coat:	Wiry and shaggy
Grooming:	Hand stripping; weekly brushing; bathing as needed, but not often
Health:	Potential joint problems; eye problems; heart defects; flea allergies
Lifespan:	13 to 14 years

Preferences:

Best Couture:	Gingham jumper and red bows
Favorite Foods:	Potato chips, pumpkin pie, candy corn
Activities:	Frisbee, witch hunting, movie night

Cavalier King Charles Spaniel

Royal Wedding in Your Future!

"Young noble seeks uncommon lady to share throne and castle."

Group: Toy

Breed Club URL: www.ackcsc.org

Profile:

This regal little spaniel can be seen in paintings as far back as the 16th century as the preferred pet of the British royalty. This charming companion has a silky, flowing coat and comes in four colors—the Blenheim (red and white), Prince Charles (tricolor), Ruby (solid red) and King Charles (black and tan). He is docile but energetic and is just as happy hiking as he is napping. He's a true family cohort, playful with kids as long as they're respectful of his small size and sensitive temperament. Though he's intelligent, he's not going to win many obedience trials, especially under the hand of a harsh trainer. He is adaptable to city or country life.

Details:

Height:	12 to 13 inches
Weight:	13 to 18 pounds
Coat:	Silky, medium length; moderate shedding
Grooming:	Weekly brushing
Health:	Ear infections; patellar luxation; congenital heart defects; eye problems
Lifespan:	9 to 11 years

Preferences:

Best Couture:	Velvet cape, of course
Favorite Foods:	Cucumber sandwiches, crumpets
Activities:	Dog shows, hunting chipmunks, polo

Chihuahua

¡Quiero Chanel y Amor!

"Soft-spoken Latin lover craves partner for dancing and more."

Group: Toy

Breed Club URL:
www.chihuahuaclubofamerica.com

Details:

Height:	6 to 8 inches
Weight:	Under 6 pounds
Coat:	Long-coated and short coated; both coat types shed seasonally
Grooming:	Weekly brushing to quell shedding
Tail:	Curled over back
Health:	Patellar luxation; eye problems; low blood sugar; congenital heart defects; tracheal collapse; heat stroke
Lifespan:	16 to 18 years

Profile:

The Chihuahua is believed by many to be the perfect underarm accessory, especially draped in rhinestones and tucked comfortably into a trendy bag. The breed originated in Mexico and has a history that dates back to the Aztecs, though there are several theories and legends surrounding the origins of the breed's early ancestors. This active, intelligent breed is easily house-trained onto newspapers or to a litter box, making him not much more difficult to care for than a cat. Many people keep two or more Chichis together, which keeps the dogs active but compounds their barking. The Chihuahua needs a great deal of socialization; he can be dog-aggressive, which puts him at a great disadvantage. This breed is not recommended for children (because of his fragility). Spoiled and sheltered Chichis also tend to become nervous biters. Always walk a Chihuahua with a body harness rather than a collar, and let Chico get some exercise despite your temptation to carry him around constantly.

Preferences:

Best Couture:	Giant hats, diamond collar, a wardrobe of sweaters and jackets, as he often gets cold.
Favorite Foods:	Pulled pork, vanilla ice cream, chalupas
Activities:	Siestas, chasing bugs and Pugs, dancing the rhumba

Chinese Crested

Let's Start Our Own Colony!

"Hot-blooded doll promises many a good-hair day!"

Group: Toy

Breed Club URL: www.chinesecrestedclub.info

Preferences:

Best Couture:	T-shirt to protect from sunburn, sweater in winter (no wool!)
Favorite Foods:	Peanut butter, yogurt, tofu
Activities:	Sunday drives, watching TV, cool dips

Details:

Height:	11 to 13 inches
Weight:	Up to 12 pounds
Coat:	Hairless variety is naked except silky hair on head, ears, feet and tail; Powderpuff variety has long, silky, fly-away hair and sheds minimally
Grooming:	Hairless variety, hand lotion daily for dry skin (no lanolin), sunscreen in the warm months, weekly bathing to avoid clogged pores, attention to scratches or cuts, nail trimming; Powderpuff variety, daily brushing
Tail:	Natural with tuft
Health:	Dental issues; skin and allergy issues; Legg-Perthes disease
Lifespan:	15 to 16 years

Profile:

If you want a lot of attention from both a dog and from strangers on the street, then the Chinese Crested is the breed for you. Bred as a companion, this dog will be your shadow, happy to bask in your presence. The breed comes in two varieties: the Hairless, with tufts of silky hair on the head, legs and tail; and the Powderpuff, with long silky hair that makes him look a little like a miniature sighthound. The Hairless actually sweats rather than pants when he's overheated. The Hairless variety is not the best choice for families with small children because the dog's skin is easily injured, though his temperament is well suited for gentle, mannerly kids. Most dogs of this size love to be carried, but the Chinese Crested is prone to tipping the scales, so let Wonton walk sometimes.

Coton de Tuléar

A Madagascan Delight!

"Exotic Islander awaits special someone to carry her umbrella."

Group: Companion Dogs (United Kennel Club)

Breed Club URL: www.usactc.org and
www.cotondogs.com

Profile:

The Coton looks like a longer-bodied Maltese made out of cotton candy! He's sweet and irresistible. As its name suggests, this French breed's fluffy topcoat is cottony and thick, and most dogs are white, though they also are seen in white/black. First established in Tuléar on the island of Madagascar, this is an ancient breed related to the Bichon Frise, Havanese and Bolognese. This "Velcro" dog is playful, alert and social, and likes nothing more than to be right in the middle of family life. Cotons are as good in apartments as they are on spacious estates, and they are extremely trainable, though many have a stubborn streak.

Details:

Height: 8½ to 12½ inches

Weight: Approx. 8 to 13 pounds

Coat: Fluffy, light, fly-away coat; sheds very little, if at all

Grooming: Daily brushing if in full coat; coat can be clipped short; bathing twice a year or when dirty

Health: No real health issues

Lifespan: 14 to 16 years

Preferences:

Best Couture: Faux mink cape, argyle ski sweater

Favorite Foods: Escargot, cured meats, rice, shrimp

Activities: Bird watching, tiki-bar-hopping

English Toy Spaniel

Just Call Me "Charlie"

"British Royal seeks scandalous playmate or casual chum."

Group: Toy

Breed Club URL: www.etsca.org

Profile:

Called the King Charles Spaniel (not to be confused with the Cavalier King Charles Spaniel) in Jolly Old England, the English Toy Spaniel is an active and cuddly cohort that is good at retrieving games, a behavior that hearkens back to his hunting-dog ancestors. His short snout and undershot jaw are said to have come from crosses with Pugs. Like the Cavalier, the breed also comes in four colors: the Blenheim (red and white), Prince Charles (tricolor), Ruby (solid red) and King Charles (black and tan). A true lapdog, the "Charlie" adores napping, eating morsels of tasty table food and entertaining his owners. Families with older children are fine for this breed, but younger children may cause him some stress. Don't let this pug-faced dog exert himself in the heat.

Details:

Height: About 10 inches

Weight: 8 to 14 pounds

Coat: Fine, silky coat

Grooming: Weekly brushing; trim feathering on feet

Health: Ear infections; luxating patella; eye problems, heart issues; heat exhaustion; breathing problems; snoring

Lifespan: 10 to 12 years

Preferences:

Best Couture: T-shirt with little angel's wings

Favorite Foods: Candied carrots, fig cookies, clotted cream

Activities: Baking, sailing, dog parks

Fox Terrier

I'm Game If You Are!

"Cleverly made hunk in pursuit of foxy Type A."

Group: Terrier

Breed Club URL: www.aftc.org

Profile:

The Wire Fox Terrier and the Smooth Fox Terrier rival only the Jack and Parson Russell Terriers in their saucy temperament, stubborn streak and assertive disposition. The Fox Terriers resulted from crosses of a variety of terriers and hounds and were used in England in the 1800s as ratters and to flush foxes from their holes. Unlikely candidates for a Gucci handbag, Fox Terriers are like sticks of dynamite beneath charming, well-bred exteriors. They love to play and bark and will readily pick fights with much larger dogs. Exercise is essential for these lively terriers, though apartment living is fine if they get out with their owners for regular long walks. For their moderate sizes, they are surprisingly strong and muscular. Keep them groomed to the nines to match your high-end couture.

Details:

Height: up to 15½ inches

Weight: up to 19 pounds

Coat: Wire has wiry, crinkly and wavy but never curly coat that sheds minimally; Smooth has smooth, flat and hard coat that sheds a bit

Grooming: Weekly brushing; Wire needs hand stripping

Health: Seizures; skin problems; joint problems; eye problems

Lifespan: 15 to 16 years

Preferences:

Best Couture: Touristy Hawaiian shirt

Favorite Foods: London broil, rabbit stew, boiled potatoes

Activities: Outdoor romps, camping, terrorizing rodents

Havanese

Heaven in Havana

"Sunny Havana muchacha longs for handsome hombre to stroll the Malacon."

Group: Toy

Breed Club URL: www.havanese.org

Profile:

The National Dog of Cuba has been developed on the island since the 16ᵗʰ century when Spanish ships brought the dogs overseas. The breed has Bichon origins and was once called the Spanish Silk Poodle in reference to his lightweight, wavy coat. For showing, the coat is occasionally corded like that of a Puli, though this isn't typical. The silky coat comes in colors including cream, gold, silver, champagne, tan, blue, black, parti-color and tricolor. He is an active, lively lapdog and can be yappy, but he is also highly trainable and eager to please. He is amiable and good with gentle children and other pets, and he loves nothing more than to cuddle up with his favorite *amigo*.

Details:

Height:	8½ to 11½ inches
Weight:	7 to 13 pounds
Coat:	Light and silky; very little shedding
Grooming:	Weekly brushing; professional grooming
Health:	Joint problems; cardiac problems
Lifespan:	12 to 14 years

Preferences:

Best Couture:	Shiny club wear
Favorite Foods:	Plaintains, shrimp, conch
Activities:	Long walks sunbathing, pedicures

Italian Greyhound

Che Bello Cane

"Slim, luscious Mediterranean lady—18-12-12—looking for friend to share romantic, lo-carb pasta meals."

Group: Toy

Breed Club URL: www.italiangreyhound.org

Profile:

This refined, spindly-legged little sighthound is a relative of the Greyhound but is proportionally *much* smaller. The breed originated in Greece, Turkey and Italy and is said to be over 2,000 years old. It was thought to have been used to hunt vermin and very small game, though it was likely bred as a companion. The IG is a family dog who prefers the indoors and gets cold easily. He can be aloof with people he doesn't know, but if he's socialized properly he can be quite gregarious. Always keep your IG on a leash, because he's likely to run off after a paper bag blowing in the wind or a passing squirrel, and he's quite quick.

Details:

Height: 13 to 15 inches

Weight: 8 to 12 pounds

Coat: Short; sheds a little

Grooming: Weekly brushing with a soft brush to remove dead hair

Health: Seizures; patellar luxation

Lifespan: 13 to 15 years

Preferences:

Best Couture: Wind-resistant jackets or warm college sweaters, doggie booties in ice or snow

Favorite Food: Pasta!

Activities: Midnight gondola rides, quiet nights at home with Andrea Boccelli's latest album

Jack and Parson Russell Terriers

Parson, the Marrying Type

"Don't let my collar fool you—I'm irreverent and profane."

Group: Terrier

Breed Club URL: www.prtaa.org

Details:

Height:	12 to 15 inches
Weight:	13 to 17 pounds
Coat:	Coarse, dense and straight; sheds
Grooming:	Daily brushing to remove dead hair
Tail:	Docked
Health:	Eye problems; joint problems; thyroid issues
Lifespan:	13 to 15 years

Profile:

A favorite in the US and UK for generations, the Jack Russell Terrier is the original pocket pooch. A tiny terrier full of piss and vinegar, small enough to fit into the horseman's saddlebag, he was released after the Foxhounds located the quarry. Recently this bright little dog was featured as the famous Skip from the movie *My Dog Skip* and as Eddie on the popular TV show *Frasier*. Long recognized by the United Kennel Club, the breed was recognized by the American Kennel Club only in 1997 as the Jack Russell Terrier. The AKC now calls the breed Parson Russell Terrier, a name change that has caused much confusion. By any name, this is a very intelligent, energetic and highly trainable dog, but he is also prone to an incredible amount of mischief and stubbornness. But, aside from losing a shoe or two, dealing with some barking at passersby and preventing him from digging his way to China from the back yard, you'll find that this dog makes a great companion, albeit a handful.

Preferences:

Best Couture:	This dog can get away with anything!
Favorite Foods:	Turkey loaf, granola bars, spray cheese
Activities:	Church picnics, long walks, chasing yummy toys

Japanese Chin

Let's Make Some Memoirs!

I'm a little Geisha with love up my sleeve."

Group: Toy

Breed Club URL: www.japanesechinonline.org

Profile:

This 1,500-year-old breed's stylish, elegant appearance attracts a lot of attention. It is said to be related to the other short-muzzled Asian breeds, such as the Shih Tzu, Pekingese and Tibetan Spaniel. Several years ago, the breed was known as the Japanese Spaniel.

The Chin is a quiet lapdog who makes a great family companion and is considered by lovers of the breed to be a "potato chip dog"—owners find it difficult to have just one. These intelligent dogs do well in organized sports, and their can-do attitude makes them a pleasure to train. They can be aloof with strangers, but they are warm and affectionate to family.

Details:

Height: 8 to 11 inches

Weight: 9 pounds

Coat: Silky and flowing

Grooming: Weekly brushing; cleaning of the facial folds

Health: Eye issues; facial fold infections

Lifespan: 10 to 12 years

Preferences:

Best Couture: Tuxedo for males, kimono or smart suit and pillbox hat for females

Favorite Foods: Whitefish burgers, edamame

Activities: Watercolor painting, slumber parties, afternoon tea

Kyi-Leo®

Meet the Queen of the Jungle

"Are you brave enough to tame this designer lion?"

Group: Companion (American Rare Breed Association)

Breed Club: Kyi-Leo® Club

Profile:

Kyi means "dog" in Tibetan, and *Leo* means "lion" in Latin. This little "lion dog" is a rare breed that derived from Maltese and Lhasa Apso crosses in the 1950s. Like their parent breeds, they are alert and make great watchdogs (but don't expect an intruder to be particularly fearful of this fluffy little poochy). They are playful and lively, and do best in an environment where they can get some exercise. They are fairly difficult to find, but worth the "lion" hunt.

Details:

Height:	8 to 12 inches
Weight:	8 to 16 pounds
Coat:	Long, silky and thick; natural part down back
Grooming:	Frequent brushing and combing to avoid matting
Tail:	Curled over the back when in motion or alert; heavily feathered
Health:	Patellar luxation (rarely)
Lifespan:	12 to 16 years

Preferences:

Best Couture:	T-shirt that reads "High Maintenance," a pair of dark K9 Doggles and a tiara
Favorite Foods:	Chicken, cheese, green beans, bananas
Activities:	Yoga, gardening, walks, socializing

Lhasa Apso

Frigid and Isolated? Who Me?

"Ex-Tibetan monk ready to let veil down and party."

Group: Non-Sporting

Breed Club URL: www.lhasaapso.org

Profile:

Friendly and spirited, this family dog loves to go everywhere with his favorite people and adapts well to new surroundings. This is a very old breed that was bred in Tibet by monks over 2,000 years ago. Apsos were considered sacred dogs who brought good luck to those who owned them. They look precious, which they are, but they also are truly hardy, playful, affectionate dogs. They don't tolerate rude children, but will adore the children of the family if they are gentle and considerate. Schedule a regular salon appointment for your Apso, as his coat is divine when in a sleek, floor-length 'do.

Details:

Height: 10 to 11 inches

Weight: 13 to 15 pounds

Coat: Long and heavy double coat

Grooming: Daily brushing

Health: Eye problems; skin problems

Lifespan: 15 to 18 years

Preferences:

Best Couture: A silk cape

Favorite Foods: Mutton kabobs, barley cakes, yak butter

Activities: Guarding your monastery, posing for sculptors

Maltese

Ever Been Touched by an Angel?

"Single-coated white Toy seeks refined gentleman to take the lead."

Group: Toy

Breed Club URL: www.americanmaltese.org

Profile:

This graceful, fine-boned, ancient breed of Malta has been depicted in artwork as early as 6000 BC, making it the oldest breed likely bred to hunt rodents. The ancient Egyptians believed that the Maltese had healing powers, and studies today confirm that petting a dog lowers blood pressure and has a calming effect. Despite the breed's diminutive size, he is a fearless dog, more than willing to protect his family or himself as the need arises. But, if socialized well, he is a cuddly and active family companion. If you want to keep his coat long and flowing, you will have to brush him every other day; another option is keeping him in a short and cute "puppy cut" by taking him regularly to the grooming salon. Some individuals are difficult to house-train, though they take well to paper training.

Details:

Height:	8 to 10 inches
Weight:	Under 7 pounds
Coat:	Long and silky; does not shed
Grooming:	Weekly brushing
Health:	Skin, eye, dental and respiratory problems; heat exhaustion
Lifespan:	12 to 15 years

Preferences:

Best Couture:	Bows, tiaras
Favorite Foods:	Soft goat cheese, meat cakes (Pastizzi)
Activities:	Pillow talk, salon visits, stalking June bugs

Miniature Dachshund

Up for a Little Badgering?

"Shortish European willing to work below or beat the bush."

Group: Hound

Breed Club URL:
www.dachshund-dca.org

Details:

Height:	About 6 inches
Weight:	11 pounds and under
Coat:	Three coat types: long and silky; short and hard; wiry and coarse
Grooming:	Weekly brushing
Tail:	Natural
Health:	Spinal disk problems; diabetes; obesity; skin issues
Lifespan:	12 to 16 years

Profile:

Only one hound goes well in a Prada bag, and that hound is the Miniature Dachshund. Originally bred in the 1700s to "go to ground" after fox, hare and weasel, the Mini Dachshund has developed into a great apartment and family dog. Hounds in general are notorious for being unfocused in training, distracted by the scent or flurry of furry animals. While training a Dachsie can present challenges, the breed certainly is trainable with patience and plenty of positive reinforcement (treats go a long way). Owners admire them for their independence and bold demeanor, and Dachsies have long been favorites in urban, suburban and rural communities. The Dachshund is a dashing clown, intelligent and home-loving. He is strong and quite capable of dispatching small pets, like the family bunny, before you can turn around to stop him. Don't let your Dachsie jump off furniture or navigate too many stairs, as joint and spinal injuries can result.

Preferences:

Best Couture:	Wiener dog costume or pirate costume (any costume, really)
Favorite Foods:	Cheese doodles, boiled meats, wiener schnitzel
Activities:	Rat digs, chasing anything that moves, midnight swims

Miniature Pinscher

High-Stepping with My Baby

"King of Toys lobbies for fresh subject."

Group: Toy

Breed Club URL: www.minpin.org

Details:

Height:	10 to 12½ inches
Weight:	8 to 11 pounds
Coat:	Short and smooth
Grooming:	Weekly wipe-down and brushing to remove dead hair
Tail:	Docked
Health:	Joint problems; leg injuries
Lifespan:	14 to 15 years

Profile:

Inquisitive and tenacious, the Min Pin is a whirlwind of a tiny dog, energetic and always into mischief. The breed was originally used as vermin hunters in stables. Aptly called the "King of Toys," the Min Pin is known for his alertness and his instant willingness to sound an alarm (often to the annoyance of your next-door neighbors). A patient and competent trainer can do a lot with the Min Pin. He is bright and an eager entertainer, and his prance-like gait is a real attention-getter. Because this breed is so curious and persistent, owners should crate-train their Min Pins or keep them in safe, contained areas when unsupervised. If a Min Pin is given a squeaky chew toy, he will do whatever it takes to remove the squeaker and may choke on it; therefore, either remove the squeakers from toys before offering them to a Min Pin or avoid squeaky toys altogether (as well as any other toys with small parts that can be removed and swallowed).

Preferences:

Best Couture:	Argyle sweater
Favorite Foods:	Turkey hotdogs, vanilla wafers, corn chips
Activities:	Beachcombing, circus tricks, eating

Miniature Schnauzer

Wanna Get Wired?

"Looking for a quarry mate who's electric and sheer fun?"

Group: Terrier

Breed Club URL: http://amsc.us

Profile:

This tireless little vermin hunter originated in Germany in the late 1800s and was bred down from the Standard Schnauzer. This dog is hyper-alert to his surroundings and though he looks great in a sweater and fits nicely in a bag, he's very heavy and muscular for his size. With the Poodle in his background, the Mini is a bright dog who's more willing to please than his British terrier counterparts. Minis are easy to train, but like all terriers they have a stubborn streak and need a creative trainer who uses positive-reinforcement methods. Some breeders are creating "teacup" Mini Schnauzers, but these aren't a separate breed or recognized size—they are just undersized.

Details:

Height:	12 to 14 inches
Weight:	11 to 20 pounds
Coat:	Coarse outer coat with soft undercoat; sheds little, if at all; people with allergies do well with schnauzers
Grooming:	Professional grooming to keep the typical schnauzer style; hand stripping; infrequent bathing
Tail:	Docked
Health:	Diabetes; pancreatitis
Lifespan:	14 to 15 years

Preferences:

Best Couture:	Sweater vests for boys, plaid jumpers for girls
Favorite Foods:	Pizza bagels, canned chicken, liverwurst
Activities:	Hiking, staring down potential meals, playing detective

Moscow Toy Terrier

From Moscow with Love

"Elegant Russian lady seeks sophisticated comrade."

Group: Companion (American Rare Breed Association)

Profile:

At a mere few pounds, the Moscow Toy Terrier would happily stow away into a matinee or roadside café, being not much larger than a Blackberry in your pocket. Known as a lady's dog in Russia, this breed makes a great apartment dog, though he tends toward chunkiness if carried more often than walked. He has an appearance slightly reminiscent of a Papillon, with fringed ears that make him look ready to flit from flower to flower. He also looks something like a tiny deer, with his big eyes and lanky limbs. This lively breed is said to be fearless, agile and highly trainable. Like martinis made from good Russian vodka, most owners can't stop at just one.

Details:

Height:	8 to 11 inches
Weight:	4½ to 11 pounds
Coat:	Two varieties: smooth-coated and long-haired; sheds somewhat
Grooming:	Smooth-coated should be brushed weekly; long-haired should be brushed daily; bathe once monthly
Tail:	Docked to a nub
Health:	No known health issues
Lifespan:	15 to 18 years

Preferences:

Best Couture:	Fur hat
Favorite Foods:	Pierogies, canned sprats, veal bologna
Activities:	Shopping, dog parks

Norfolk Terrier

Corner a Demon in the Field

"Tired of chasing and tackling frisky vermin—this chap is ready to settle down."

Group: Terrier

Breed Club URL: www.norwichandnorfolkterrier.org

Profile:

Dogs don't get much cuter than the Norfolk Terrier, with his drop ears and expressive eyes. This stout, strong, little bundle of energy was originally used in England in the 1800s as a ratter and to rout foxes out of their holes. Don't mistake this button nosed pooch for a toy dog: he is small, but he's 100% sporting terrier, still able to do the work of his forebears. He loves to run and dig, but does well with apartment life if exercised regularly. This breed is fairly trainable, but loses focus easily and must be kept motivated. He is active and lively and is good with gentle children.

Details:

Height:	9 to 10 inches
Weight:	11 to 12 pounds
Coat:	Wiry and shaggy; light shedding
Grooming:	Weekly brushing; hand stripping twice yearly
Tail:	Docked
Health:	Not many health issues; joint problems; seizures
Lifespan:	12 to 16 years

Preferences:

Best Couture:	Preppy sweater vest
Favorite Foods:	Hamburgers, sausage, spareribs
Activities:	Barbeques, cheese-sampling parties, the beach

Norwich Terrier

No Frills, No Fuss, No Tofu

"Easy and happy-go-lucky guy seeks girl who can cook."

Group: Terrier

Breed Club URL:
www.norwichandnorfolkterrier.org

Profile:

This foxy little terrier is similar to the Norfolk, but he has prick ears rather than drop ears. He is a very sensitive creature that does well with a gentle and patient trainer. He loves his human family and is very interested in being part of the pack. The Norwich Terrier needs a job to do besides just looking cute and perky. He's adaptable, trainable and lovable, making a super companion for a girl on the go. Remember the crazy terrier fanatics in the movie *Best in Show*? Their dog, Winky, was a Norwich. If you call a breeder and want to be taken seriously, make sure to pronounce the breed name correctly: *Nor-itch.*

Details:

Height:	Under 10 inches
Weight:	About 12 pounds
Coat:	Wiry and shaggy; light shedding
Grooming:	Weekly brushing; hand stripping twice yearly
Tail:	Docked
Health:	Not many health issues; joint problems; seizures
Lifespan:	12 to 16 years

Preferences:

Best Couture:	Tweed coat
Favorite Foods:	Grilled cheese with bacon, potpies, plain bacon
Activities:	Dude ranches, guarding the family cat, chasing the same

Papillon

Lighter than Paris Herself

"Madame Butterfly seeks to net a military daddy."

Group: Toy

Breed Club URL:
www.papillonclub.org

Height:	8 to 11 inches
Weight:	7 to 10 pounds
Coat:	Medium-length, silky hair; sheds
Grooming:	Needs brushing once or twice a week
Tail:	Feathered and held over the back (the French sometimes call him "Squirrel Dog" for his flittery tail)
Health:	Joint, eye, dental and liver problems
Lifespan:	13 to 16 years

Profile:

This elegant French breed may have Spanish descendants but, since it's one of the oldest breeds, its lineage is questionable. Nevertheless, the Papillon has long been a popular toy breed and was the favored dog of Marie Antoinette, who carried her beloved pooches on her final walk to the guillotine (the dogs lived on to eat cake, though their owner didn't). Antoinette is also said to have named the breed, obviously after its butterfly-like appearance and demeanor (*papillon* means "butterfly" in French). Though the ears make this breed look ready to fly off to the nearest flower, there is also a drop-eared variety called the Phalene (which means "moth" in French), which is much less common. Descended from brilliant spaniel types, the Papillon is a star student in obedience classes and a top competitor in obedience trials. The breed can be tough to house-train but will eventually learn the ropes; Papillons have small bladders and thus should have access to a potty area every couple of hours. Though the Pap is a great family dog, he's often called the "little tyrant" because he can be possessive and bossy, but the good in this breed far outweighs the naughty.

Preferences:

Best Couture:	Nothing! This French beauty prefers to go *au naturel.*
Favorite Foods:	Pastry shells, veal sausage, croissants
Activities:	Park visits, hunting squirrels, playing fetch

Pekingese

A Most Distinctive Roll!

"Flat-faced, heavy-boned girl promises sweet fortune!"

Group: Toy

Breed Club URL:
www.geocities.com/Heartland/3843

Profile:

This imperial bouffant-with-feet has waddled his way into the hearts of people all over the world. The Peke's legendary origin is as colorful as his character: a lion fell in love with a marmoset monkey and asked that the Buddha make him small enough to join with his ladylove, resulting in the Pekingese. An ancient breed dating back more than 2,000 years, the Peke's giant head, poofball shape, intense eyes and profuse coat of many colors make him instantly recognizable. His characteristic waddle comes from his bowed legs, bred into the dog so that he wouldn't wander too far from the Chinese emperor and his harem. He's a confident and stubborn dog, not much for training, but he makes a heartwarming companion for an owner who's willing to baby him on an hourly basis.

Details:

Height: 6 to 9 inches

Weight: Up to 14 pounds

Coat: Long and thick

Grooming: Daily brushing; professional grooming every 2 to 3 months

Health: Prone to eye problems and injuries; spinal problems; patellar luxation

Lifespan: 13 to 15 years

Preferences:

Best Couture: Silk vests or pajama tops

Favorite Foods: Duck wontons, oranges, quail eggs

Activities: *Dynasty* reruns, harassing the help, massages

Pomeranian

You'll Have a Ball!

"Outgoing, shapely cheerleader has pompoms for right sporty contender."

Group: Toy

Breed Club URL:
www.americanpomeranianclub.org

Profile:

The Pom belongs to the spitz family of dogs, all of which were bred to live in the cold northern climates. They originated in northeastern Germany in a region formerly known as Pomerania, and Queen Victoria is credited for naming the breed. Many famous people have owned Poms, including Chopin, Sir Isaac Newton and Michelangelo.

The foxy little Pomeranian always has a smile on his face, making him look happy even when he's yapping at friends and strangers. Alert and curious, he makes a great watchdog; despite his size, his intensity and loyalty cannot be questioned. A Pom needs a firm but gentle trainer and a very secure yard, as Poms are accomplished escape artists. Even though they are small, they love to romp and play and they need quite a bit of exercise, which they can get simply from playing in the house or fenced yard.

Details:

Height:	8 to 11 inches
Weight:	3 to 7 pounds
Coat:	Thick; sheds a little
Grooming:	Twice-weekly brushing
Health:	Tooth and gum problems; fur loss with age
Lifespan:	13 to 17 years

Preferences:

Best Couture:	Sundresses for girls, jerseys for boys
Favorite Foods:	Tuna fish, oyster crackers in tomato soup
Activities:	Picnics, road trips, edible paints

Poodle

Splash in the Pan!

"Let's get wet and wild...a lady's man who likes fowl play."

Group: Toy/Non-Sporting

Breed Club URL:
www.poodleclubofamerica.org

Details:

Height:	Toy: 10 inches or under; Miniature: over 10 inches but no more than 15 inches
Weight:	Toy: 6 to 8 pounds Mini: 15 to 17 pounds
Coat:	Curly; does not shed; people with allergies do well with Poodles
Grooming:	Regular brushing and trips to the grooming salon
Health:	Seizures; patellar luxation; joint problems
Lifespan:	15 to 18 years

Profile:

The smallest of the Poodles, the Toy Poodle is bred down from the larger-sized Poodles, originally bred in Germany and known as the "Pudel" or "puddle dog" because of the breed's love of water. He is the official dog of France and is informally called the French Poodle, though that is not his official breed name. He is intelligent, fearless and alert, and he must be socialized very well so that his natural love of people shines through. Poodles are highly trainable; they do well in organized sports and are capable of learning many fun tricks. You might recall circus Poodles in tutus, walking on their hind legs on rolling balls. They are not great for families with small children, though they are affectionate family dogs that love nothing more than being with their favorite humans. The tiny toys and teacups in this breed are extremely small and are likely to have health problems. Owners are wise to purchase from breeders who do not breed excessively small toys. On a fun note, you can probably get away with coloring your Poodle pink or blue (and not have people think that you're *too* nuts), so stock up on some Kool-Aid, which doubles as great Poodle hair dye.

Preferences:

Best Couture:	Tutu and tiara for girls; beret and neck scarf for boys
Favorite Foods:	Escargot, Brie
Activities:	Perms, spying on ducks, dressing up

Pug

I'm a Lot to Handle!

"Don't let my name, size or grunt fool you—I'm all about passion."

Group: Toy

Breed Club URL: www.pugs.org

Profile:

The Chinese Pug relies on beauty being in the eye of the beholder. He's considered "ugly cute" by most, with his cobby body, short snout and large globular eyes, but he's a VIP in the eyes of those who fancy him. The Pug dates back to about 150 BC and has had many famous and important fans, most notably Josephine Bonaparte (Napoleon's wife), the Duke and Duchess of Windsor, Andy Warhol and Princess Grace Kelly. The Pug can be a snob and as lazy as a lump of cheese, but he wasn't bred to be anything other than a companion. He will bark when he hears noise, but he isn't going to try very hard to ward off intruders. Pugs are known to get porky and they do need exercise, but owners must be aware that Pugs can become very ill from exercising in the heat.

Details:

Height: 10 to 11 inches

Weight: 14 to 18 pounds

Coat: Smooth, medium-length; sheds mercilessly

Grooming: Weekly brushing to remove dead hair

Health: Breathing and eye problems; heat stroke

Lifespan: 12 to 14 years

Preferences:

Best Couture: Belted leather coat, anything dignified—no tutus or bikinis, please

Favorite Foods: Everything!

Activities: Bus trips, guarding pillows, terrorizing house plants

Russian Tsvetnaya Bolonka

Mail Order Bride

"Here comes your dream poochsky, all dressed in white."

Group: Companion
(American Rare Breed Association)

Breed Club URL:
www.tsvetnayabolonka.homestead.com

Profile:

If you like the Havanese and Maltese, you'll love the Tsvetnaya Bolonka. This scruffy little moppet was developed in the 1950s by crossing existing small breeds like the Bichon Frise, Shih Tzu, Poodle, Lhasa Apso, Bolognese, Pekingese and small terriers, as well as various small fluffy dogs of uncertain origin. In Russian, *bolonka* means "lap dog," which offers some insight into this dog's companion-ability. He is protective over his home and family, but given his small size won't quite be able to ward off intruders. He is affectionate and not easily excitable, making him a good dog for families with kids and senior citizens. Finding one of these classic-age designer dogs becomes the real problem, as there are not many breeders currently in the United States.

Details:

Height:	8 to 10 inches
Weight:	8 to 10 pounds
Coat:	Thick, dense, silky and curly with a well-developed undercoat; resistant to matting
Grooming:	Daily brushing of the face and tail; weekly brushing of the body; trimming or pulling of the area around the face
Health:	No known health issues
Lifespan:	15 to 16 years

Preferences:

Best Couture:	Light cable-knit sweater, bunny bathrobe
Favorite Foods:	Stewed pork (tushonka), herring fillet
Activities:	Garden parties, classical concerts

Schipperke

Hey, Sailor!

"On shore for 24 hours and looking for a little Flemish fun."

Group: Non-Sporting

Breed Club URL: www.schipperkeclub-usa.org

Preferences:

Best Couture: Sailor's outfit

Favorite Food: Belgian waffles, honey cakes, mashed potatoes

Activities: Yachting, herding the family, fishing

Details:

Height: 10 to 13 inches

Weight: 12 to 18 pounds

Coat: Thick double coat; doesn't shed until the coat "blows" seasonally two or three times a year, when shedding is considerable

Grooming: Weekly once-over; daily during shedding times

Tail: None

Health: Joint problems; eye problems; seizures

Lifespan: 14 to 16 years

Profile:

This fox-like little black dog was used in Belgium in the 1800s as a vermin hunter and watchdog on canal boats. He does very well around the water and is super-alert, ready to bark at the slightest disturbance (much to the disdain of close neighbors). This "little skipper" is constantly in turbo overdrive and needs a secure yard or a tireless owner to go for regular long walks with him. A patient and firm trainer can get a lot out of this little dog. Unlike the other small dogs we've discussed, the Schipperke derives from herding dogs and needs real activity to keep him sailing clear.

Toy Fox Terrier

Foxy and Hot to Trot!

"Eager to please tot hunts for willing game."

Group: Toy

Breed Club URL: www.atftc.com

Profile:

Courageous and loyal, the Toy Fox Terrier, once called the American Toy Terrier, makes a great indoor dog. Originally bred as a vermin hunter, he was developed in the 1930s in the US using Smooth Fox Terriers, Chihuahuas, Italian Greyhounds and Toy Manchester Terriers. As a companion, he is friendly yet protective, smart yet stubborn and highly trainable. Some individuals can become yappy, and most will be spirited and lively until old age—people will think that your 12-year-old dog is just a puppy! This tot's animation and energy give you the impression that he's a wind-up toy; of course, this toy dog is much more than a toy, and he showers his owner with devotion and "an endless abiding love."

Details:

Height:	8½ to 11½ inches
Weight:	4 to 7 pounds
Coat:	Short; sheds moderately
Grooming:	Weekly brushing to remove dead hair
Tail:	Docked
Health:	Joint problems; seizures; allergies
Lifespan:	13 to 14 years

Preferences:

Best Couture:	Fleece coat, anything that won't hinder the dog's movement—he's always on the go
Favorite Foods:	Braised carrots, bologna, mac 'n cheese
Activities:	Hiking, biking, chasing twitchy offenders

Toy Manchester Terrier

Dig an Old-Fashioned Guy?

"Small-framed black and tan ready for cocktails and good chatter."

Group: Toy

Breed Club URL:
http://clubs.akc.org/mtca/index.htm

Profile:

An energetic and intelligent watchdog, the Toy Manchester Terrier adapts to city or rural living and is often a one-person dog. Standard Manchester Terriers were used as ratters in 16th-century England, and the toy variety was bred down from the standard, which can weigh up to 22 pounds. The Toy Manchester can be bossy with other dogs and needs to be well socialized and trained. He doesn't do well in a household that's too lenient with him. This active little dog enjoys exercise but can suffer from heat exhaustion if out in the sun too long.

Details:

Height: 8 to 13 inches

Weight: 12 pounds or under

Coat: Smooth and short; sheds

Grooming: Weekly brushing to remove dead hair

Tail: Natural

Health: Joint, skin and eye problems

Lifespan: 14 to 18 years

Preferences:

Best Couture: Berber coat

Favorite Foods: Boiled beef, candy corn, broccoli

Activities: Garden parties, a good dig

West Highland White Terrier

Hardy, Urban and Pure White

"Uptown gal seeks downtown bad boy for lonely weekends."

Group: Terrier

Breed Club URL: www.westieclubamerica.com

Profile:

Westies are descendants of the Cairn Terrier and the Scottish Terrier, both of which occasionally produce white puppies in a litter. The breed was developed as a hunting companion in the 1800s in Scotland. This alert dog is great with respectful kids, but he isn't a knockabout kind of dog. He is sweet and affectionate but becomes very protective of the household and family. Like the other terriers, he is independent and can be stubborn, but can be highly trainable with positive reinforcement from a patient, loving handler. Keep his coat bright white, properly sculpted and dignified. A Westie should never look ratty, dingy or scruffy.

Details:

Height: 10 to 11 inches

Weight: 15 to 22 pounds

Coat: Coarse and wiry; sheds a little; people with allergies do well with Westies

Grooming: Weekly brushing; hand stripping; clipping around face; do not bathe often

Health: Food and flea allergies

Lifespan: 12 to 15 years

Preferences:

Best Couture: Plaid pea coat

Favorite Foods: Diner food: omelets, cheeseburgers and waffles

Activities: Dog parks, weekends in the country

Xoloitzcuintti

Show Me!

"Curvy Aztec princess seeks aristocrat to worship her."

Group: Sighthounds and Pariahs (United Kennel Club)

Breed Club URL: www.xoloworld.com

Preferences:

Best Couture:	Cotton sweater (only when outside)
Favorite Foods:	Corn tlaxcalli (tortillas), guacamole, porridge
Activities:	Sunbathing, coursing rabbits and other runaways

Details:

Height:	Toy: up to and including 13 inches
Weight:	About 12 pounds
Coat:	Hairless variety: none; coated variety: short- to medium-length single coat
Grooming:	Hairless variety needs weekly bathing to avoid skin eruptions; regular cleaning of the feet, which have active sweat glands; daily wipe-down and application of lotion (no lanolin); regular ear cleaning; sunscreen in bright sunlight; Coated variety needs moderate brushing
Health:	Skin problems; patellar luxation; dental problems
Lifespan:	15 to 17 years

Profile:

The Xoloitzcuintli *(show-low-eats-queen-tlay)*, also called the Mexican Hairless (so much more pronounceable) comes in three sizes, standard, miniature and toy. Of course, we're concerned with the toy variety. The Xolo's naked skin is surprisingly tough, though he can suffer cuts easily. This ancient breed was used as food by Pre-Columbian peoples, and the Aztecs used him for religious sacrifice. Luckily for the breed, its days on the dinner table and altar are over and he's worshipped in homes all around North America. The breed is an alert watchdog, easy to train, and thrives on human attention. He is likely to love veggies, so treat him with carrots and other healthy items rather than commercial snacks. A small version of the Xolo called the Techichi is said to be behind the origin of the Chihuahua.

Yorkshire Terrier

Desperately Seeking a New Beau

"Endless love and locks to entangle right guy for my topknot"

Group: Toy

Breed Club URL: www.ytca.org

Profile:

A terrier bred originally to hunt rodents, the Yorkie has gone from the farm to the fabulous. Originally a barn ratter, this breed is now a pampered Park Avenue pooch. He comes from Yorkshire in the North of England, where he was developed in the mid-19th century. Today he is not just one of the most popular little dogs but one of the most popular dogs of all sizes, seen everywhere from the country to the suburbs to the purse carried by Manhattan columnist and socialite Cindy Adams. Breeders have "downsized" the Yorkie over the years, making him a true pocket pup. He is affectionate, courageous, adaptable and elegant in his blue and tan locks. Take care to keep his hair out of his eyes by either clipping it or tying it up in a topknot. No Yorkie is fully dressed without a red or blue bow!

Details:

Height: 6 to 7 inches

Weight: Under 7 pounds

Coat: Long, straight, glossy and silky; doesn't shed

Grooming: Daily brushing to avoid mats (unless clippered short)

Tail: Docked

Health: Eye problems; dental problems

Lifespan: 12 to 15 years

Preferences:

Best Couture: Anything glamorous—Yorkies can pull anything off

Favorite Foods: Stinky cheese (Stilton, perhaps), butterscotch pudding

Activities: Gardening, daydreaming, stealing hearts

POCKET-POOCH DESIGNER DOGS

The pocket pooch *du jour* is anything "poo." Otherwise known as "doodle dogs," these Poodle mixes are extremely *poo*-pular with people who want a small, well-behaved, hypoallergenic (or less-allergenic) dog. You can get a little Maltipoo, Cockapoo, Schnoodle, Doxipoo or just about any other cross that a breeder has in mind. There's a lot of controversy about these dogs. High demand for them has resulted in backyard breeders' indiscriminately propagating them and charging more than for purebred pups. With that in mind, it's fair to say that there are some very responsible people producing doodle dogs, but it takes careful research and reference-checking to find one.

Puggles, for example, enjoyed a rage of attention during the designer-dog craze. The Puggle is an unlikely cross between a Pug and a Beagle, which as a tiny puppy looks like a mini-Mastiff baby. Even though the puppies start out small and cute, they can reach 30 pounds! You do not want to lug around a 30-pound Puggle in your PuchiBag, so if you want a pocket pooch, you should look for an adult Puggle who won't snap the straps of your shoulder tote. This mix can also be a little difficult to train, considering that the two parent breeds aren't out there scooping up top honors in the obedience ring.

Mixes have the benefit of being hardy and having fewer congenital problems, though you have no guarantees. The real issue is lack of consistency—one puppy could be hypoallergenic, while another puppy in the same litter will cause allergies. There are temperament and size issues as well. Buyer, beware!

Choosing and Acclimating a Pocket Pooch

O nce you've decided upon your perfect breed, you've got to find your perfect pup. Look for a reputable hobby breeder or a knowledgeable breed fancier, someone who loves the breed and is devoted to ensuring that the breed improves with each generation. A puppy's sire (father) and dam (mother) have a major influence on how your pup will behave, as does the person who bred the pup. A good breeder tests his dogs for genetic issues and makes judicious pairings as a result of the tests. The pups are socialized to humans at a very young age and receive the best healthcare available. A good breeder interviews potential owners at length to make sure that each puppy is being placed in a good home. A good breeder should agree to always take back a dog if the new owner can't keep him, at any time during the life of the dog (but don't look for your money back). Reputable breeders of this sort range from those with large kennels to individuals with just a few dogs who breed only a litter or two each year. The American Kennel Club maintains a listing of breed clubs and breeder referral contacts, which is a great place to start. Check it out at www.akc.org in the "Future Dog Owners" section.

THINGS TO DISCUSS WITH A BREEDER

- *How long have you been involved in the breed?* Ideally, the breeder should have been in the breed for many years and is perhaps also involved in showing his dogs. Most serious breeders show their dogs.
- *Why do you love this breed?* The breeder should be passionate about the breed and excited to tell you all kinds of details about its history that you probably didn't know (and maybe didn't need or want to know!).
- *What other breeds do you have?* If the breeder is involved with too many breeds, it's likely that he is in it for the money, not for the good of the dogs. However, many breeders are interested in similar-type dogs, so if someone says they breed Shih Tzu, Lhasa Apsos and Pugs, perhaps they have a strong interest in the Asian breeds. Other breeders may breed two or three terrier breeds or perhaps have a large breed and a small breed in their kennel.
- *When I visit, can I see the litter's parents and your other dogs?* Any breeder who doesn't want you to see at least one of the parent dogs has something to hide. However, some breeders do send their dogs out with handlers for showing, and breeders often co-own dogs with other breeders, so it is conceivable that the sire wouldn't be on the premises. However, the dam should be on the premises with the puppies. You won't see any female dog at a show who had a litter of pups five to eight weeks earlier.
- *Do the puppies have pedigrees?* The breeder should have registered the puppies with the AKC (or, in the case of a rare breed, with the UKC, ARBA or another recognized registry) and should be able to tell you about the pups' lineage and show you their pedigree. Mixed-breed puppies are not eligible for registration.
- *What titles do the parents have?* Most breeders will try to put conformation or obedience titles on their dogs, so it's a good sign if the parents have won titles in dog shows. You should see titles in the pup's pedigree in the names of his parents and ancestors, championship certificates displayed on the breeder's walls and lots of ribbons from past shows.
- *Do you work on correcting genetic problems in the breed?* The breeder shouldn't deny that genetic issues exist in the breed, as they exist in most every breed. A good breeder has relevant health testing done and won't breed a dog that shows signs of or tests positive for a genetic disorder.
- *How many litters do you breed each year?* Usually, hobby breeders have one to three litters a year. Whelping and raising puppies is very time- and labor-intensive

(although for reputable breeders it is a labor of love), and a good breeder will want to take the time to socialize and place the puppies well. Since toy-dog breeds have smaller litters and require less space than larger dogs, it's possible that a breeder will have more breeding dogs on the premises and will have four or more litters per year, but too many litters per year is a warning sign. If the breeder brags about how many litters he produces, he is likely in it for the money and not too concerned about the pups' or the parents' well-being. Do more research into the breeder's program or move on to another breeder.

- *How are your puppies socialized?* There's a very short window of socialization time for a puppy, so the breeder should make the most of it by handling the pups, letting other people handle them, introducing them to new sights and sounds and, in general, teaching the puppies about the world beyond the whelping box.

- *When can I bring the puppy home?* Puppies generally are ready to leave their mothers at about eight to ten weeks old, but toy-dog breeders will want to keep their pups a little longer to give them some more time to grow and to make sure that they're eating well and have the proper vaccinations. It's not uncommon for a breeder of toy dogs to keep puppies until they are 12 or 14 weeks of age. A breeder who wants to send a pup home before eight weeks isn't worth patronizing.

- *What does your health guarantee entail?* Every puppy should come with a health guarantee to ensure that the pup is healthy when he goes home with you and remains healthy for a specified time period. You may have to take the pup to be checked by a veterinarian within a certain time frame in order for the health guarantee to be valid.

- *What do I have to do in order to get this puppy?* Good question! The breeder will probably want you to enter into a neuter/spay contract stating that you will "fix" the dog as soon as he or she is old enough. Ideally you found a breeder within a reasonable distance from your home so that you were able to go for a visit and will be able to pick up your puppy when the time comes. In rarer breeds, where breeders and puppies are not numerous, some breeders will ship pups by plane, conditions permitting. Remember that little dogs get stressed and cold easily, so shipping isn't ideal.

- *Do you participate in rescue for your breed?* Most serious breeders who adore their breed will actively participate in breed rescue, whether it's fostering and placing homeless dogs or raising money for the parent club's rescue program.

- *What kinds of clothes do your dogs prefer?* Just kidding! Don't ask this—you're likely to get a blank stare. Most breeders don't stock designer wardrobes for their dogs.

you pick up your pup. There will be plenty of time to shop and show off later. Your puppy's homecoming sets the tone for the start of your relationship. Here are a few tips to get you started:

• Make an appointment ahead of time with a veterinarian for a health check. Yes, it's the drudgery that comes with owning a dog, but everyone has to do it. Actually, most people can't wait to get their new pup to the doc to make sure that little Muffin is healthy and to get much-needed advice on keeping her that way.

• Stock up on all of the puppy essentials before the big arrival. Yes, shopping! Get what you need before you pick Betsy up from the breeder. Have her bed in place, her blankies and toys where she can get them, the baby gates and/or crate set up, her bowls exactly in the spot where she will use them and her food in the cabinet. Of course you will have already picked out a stylish collar and leash (or two, or three) with a sparkly ID tag. Shopping is fun, but after she comes home you'll want to spend your time bonding with your precious new addition.

- Bring the puppy directly home from the breeder. Said it before, going to say it again—there will be time for showing off later. For now, pup needs to get to a quiet, safe place where she can settle in.
- Keep all other pets out of the way during the pup's introduction to the household. Your puppy's first couple of hours in the home should be as uneventful as possible. If you have another dog, keep him away from the new pup for now, and introduce them later in the day in a neutral area, not in the established dog's territory.
- Offer the puppy bottled water only, or fill up bottles with water from the place where the pup is coming from so that you can offer him what his stomach is used to; this is done to avoid any intestinal problems. Think of your puppy like a rock star—that mineral water is in the *contract*.
- Don't put him on the couch or bed, because a fall can cause a serious accident. A pocket poochie puppy is easily injured and won't think twice about leaping off a couch to get to you—he lacks the experience to know that gymnastics aren't a good idea at his age.

- Don't bathe the pup unless he gets very stinky. The first bath should be at about four months of age unless something messy happens. Sure, it's tempting to snap a pic of Fifi the Poodle in the tub surrounded by suds, but it's not necessary. Excessive bathing can dry out sensitive puppy skin.
- Never hold the puppy by the scruff of the neck. Yes, the mother dog does this, but you aren't the mother dog. Holding a pup by the scruff is seen as a reprimand and is likely to scare the pup.

• Start a house-training schedule and stick to it. Realize that puppy's bladder is very small and he needs to "go" very frequently. You have to really devote yourself to house-training your new pup. A lot of people choose to begin with paper training for a small dog, which is fine as long as you stick to it.

• Block off the pup's access to stairways. Invest in puppy gates to set limits in the household. Allowing your new puppy full access to the house is like allowing a teenage girl full access to the mall with an unlimited credit

Ten Tips for Choosing a Healthy Pup

1. The puppy should be alert and playful. However, you might arrive for a visit with the breeder to find a litter of napping pups that have been playing all day. Don't discount them as ill just because they're tired. If they're sleeping when you arrive, make an appointment for another time so you can see them when they are wide awake.
2. The nose should be cool and damp.
3. The eyes should be free of discharge and free of white spots and scratches.
4. Healthy gums are pink, not whitish. Dentition and bite should be appropriate for the breed; teeth do not correct as the pup grows.
5. The ears should be clean and free of odor.
6. Healthy puppies are often plump, but a distended belly can indicate worms or other digestive problems. Also beware of rail-thin puppies.
7. The fur shouldn't be patchy, and the skin should be free of scabbing and sores.
8. The puppy should move easily without limping, though some puppies in some breeds are more awkward than others. Small-breed puppies generally look like scaled-down versions of the adult dogs and should move four-square.
9. The belly button should be healed. A bulge could indicate a hernia.
10. The rear end should be clean, not soiled, irritated or red; stools should be firm.

card. Set limits! Allow puppy to explore the house with supervision. Follow the pup around and watch him sniff in the corners and jump around the table legs—but really *watch*. You're going to have to stop him from chewing wires and finding a potty spot under the dining room table.

- Start getting him used to being inside a crate. If you're going to crate-train your pup, and most people should, start familiarizing him with the crate from day one. Don't coddle and baby him the first few nights, thinking that's what he needs. It's just going to make crate training a lot harder.

- Don't let children over-handle him. Puppies need a good deal of rest. Young kids might treat the pup like a toy. Well, Buster might be a toy breed, but he's not going to take well to little Timmy trying to open his battery pack.

- If you take him outside before he has all of his vaccinations, don't put him down on the ground. There are all kinds of nasties on the sidewalks and in the grass that can make your pup ill. Follow your veterinarian's advice

on when it will be safe to allow little Binky to walk the streets on his own four feet.

PANIC ATTACKS, TANTRUMS AND SHEER BOREDOM

Is Kammando, your slightly high-strung Chinese Crested, pulling out his hair when you leave him alone in the house? Is this behavior a panic attack or a performance-art vehicle for your sleepy cat? Most likely, this display of flying hair and back flips is a result of separation anxiety. This happens when you leave the house and Kammando becomes distressed by your absence and tries to comfort himself with

distracting and ultimately disturbing behaviors. Even the cat finds these behaviors alarming! Your dog may resort to destroying your stuff, ingesting the fur from his tail and your bear rug, scratching at the door or your antique secretarial, piddling on your now-hairless bear rug and so forth. A dog can work himself up into such an unattractive state with barking, howling and whining that you won't even recognize him. Worse, he can become aggressive, and some say spiteful (though he's really not acting out of spite, just nerves).

Generally speaking, separation anxiety can happen in dogs who were separated too early from their mothers, didn't get enough interaction as a puppy, spent too much time in a kennel or shelter, have been shuffled from home to home or have been getting less attention because of a new job, new baby, illness in the family or other reason. Of course, spoiled rotten toy dogs, those who haven't had enough discipline and routine in their lives, can experience separation anxiety by being placed in their crates for ten minutes. Often, bored dogs show separation anxiety behaviors, but the difference

between an anxious dog and a bored dog is that the anxious dog will show the same behaviors every time you leave, while a bored dog will find different ways to amuse himself. Small dogs that are bred to be companions don't like to be alone and can show some signs of separation anxiety if leaving the house is not handled properly. Most of the damage that happens in the home will take place immediately after you leave. Keeping that in mind, you have to give the dog something to do at the time of your departure.

Try this: stuff a rubber toy with kibble mixed with wet food, then stuff a piece of dried liver, cheese or something else that's nice and stinky in the end to keep the food from falling out and then put the toy into the freezer. Each day when you leave, give the dog the toy (you'll need a few of them). Ideally, he will be so distracted with getting the food out that he won't have time to worry about your leaving the house. You can also give him a sturdy chew bone or long-lasting treat, or scatter some food on the floor as you leave. The dog must start eating before you go—some dogs get so

Accessorizing Your Pocket Pooch

Accessorizing sounds fun, but it's also practical. Brandy needs quite a lot of swag to keep her happy, safe and stylin'. This chapter shows you how to properly choose the basics and beyond. Hold on to your purses, ladies (and gents), as some of these items can be very pricey. Is there anything too luxurious for your pampered furbaby?

CRATE

The crate is an essential tool for house-training and for keeping your puppy safe and out of trouble. It's not a prison! When used properly, it will be a comfortable den that your dog will enjoy spending time in. The crate should be just large enough for your pocket pooch to stand up in, turn around in and snuggle up on a comfy blanket or mat. It might be tempting to buy a large crate and outfit it like a home—resist the urge, no matter how much fun ordering little furniture would be! Your pup should not use the crate as a place to eat or eliminate. He doesn't need a dinette or bidet in his crate. The good news is that there are many fashionable small crates on the market, so you don't have to suffer an ugly plastic monstrosity in your living room. If a crate is a little too passé for your trendy pup, you can try a portable doggie crib with a zip-up top.

EXERCISE PEN

If you don't want to use a crate and you have enough space, you can use an exercise pen ("ex-pen").

This is a foldable and portable pen, made of hinged panels of sturdy wire mesh, that comes in different heights and can be set up in different configurations to create an area of safe confinement. You can even buy a top and a floor for Peewee's pen. It's also fun saying "Ex-pen!" since it makes you sound like a superhero! Ideally, the area should be large enough to include a small crate, a bed, a water dish and newspaper as a toilet area.

PUPPY GATE

Another option for keeping Little Lulu contained is a puppy gate, which you can get at any well-stocked pet shop (or toy/children's store, where they call them "baby gates"). These are the same devices designed to keep two-legged crawlers and toddlers from accessing rooms with breakable things or the danger zones (bathrooms, utility rooms, etc.). You will use them to keep your dog contained in a safe area with a durable, washable, non-slip floor. You'll have to "puppy proof" this area to make sure that Tuffy doesn't get into anything he shouldn't.

FOOD AND WATER BOWLS

Little dogs get to choose from many fun and functional bowls. Ceramic, stainless steel and heavy plastic are all good choices. Stainless steel lasts longest, and since little dogs live a long time, you might as well invest in quality dishes. Choose a weighted bowl, especially for water, or one with a wide, non-skid bottom. You can also place his bowl on a non-skid mat. This keeps the dog from nosing the bowl around the kitchen and making a mess, not to mention that these mats come in many adorable designs.

COLLAR AND HARNESS

Most dog trainers recommend training with a flat nylon collar, and though these are okay for the larger of the small breeds, most little dogs should be walked with a harness. There are some very attractive soft harnesses on the market that are made just for small dogs. They fit around the body so that there are no pressure points to make the dog uncomfortable. Choke and prong collars should never be used on little dogs.

The collar you use will probably be just for decoration and identification. If Fifi's thing is lots of bling-bling, she's in luck—dog collars come studded with crystals, gems and even real diamonds. If little Bruiser wouldn't be caught dead in diamonds, there are spiked collars made just for him. Make sure that the collar fits snugly enough so that you can put just two fingers between it and the dog's neck. If your pup isn't there when you're buying the collar, measure his neck circumference at home and then add one

Chew and Bark Jacobs plush shoe toys, as well as her plush Sniffany's box and her Chewy Vuitton. For your purse's sake, you'll be glad to know that Jimmy, Marc, Louis and the folks at Tiffany's don't actually manufacture dog toys.

BED

Mahogany and maple, canopy and memory foam, four-poster, toile and Burberry—if you can dream it, a dog-bed manufacturer has probably already made it. It seems that all of the top designers are getting wise to the discriminating dog owner's need for chic dog gear. Beds for little dogs have gotten extremely fancy, and your doll deserves to slumber in true comfort. Sure, Fido will snooze and snore just as well in the standard doughnut-shaped bolster bed, but wouldn't a Victorian silk divan look divine in your townhouse? Don't have a lot of space? Get a doggie-sized Murphy bed. Depending on your price range, you can buy anything from a simple pillow to a doggie-sized couch with removable slipcovers. Make sure that any doggie bed you buy is machine washable or has a washable cover.

JEWELRY AND HAIR ACCESSORIES

It's true that money can buy you a pretty good dog, but it can't buy you the wag of the tail. However, Lola will certainly be wagging when you outfit her with a rhinestone pendant. Well, she's probably wagging because you, her beloved owner, are putting the ritz on her, but who's splitting hairs here? No, dogs don't *need* jewelry, but any girl worth her weight in Swarovski crystals knows that even a doggie's face is fetchingly framed by a charming chain and charms. Now say that three times fast!

If you like to keep Chloe's hair long on top and you like to see her eyes every now and then, you'll need some hair ties and barrettes. You can get as fancy as crystals, bows, pearls and feathers, or you can go with a simple no-snag latex band made specifically for hair.

STROLLERS AND SNUGGLIES

Just because Sunny is a Shih Tzu doesn't mean that he's not really *your baby*. Strollers for dogs are becoming popular for the toy-dog set. Power walkers and city dwellers need to be able to rock and roll, and if Champ can't keep up, then he's got to be carried or driven. Gone are the days of the dog's being pulled in the Little Red Flyer wagon by the *Little Rascals* gang. Today, you can stroll in style with a stroller designed for dogs—most allow you to zip the dog inside and can be adapted to handle two or more (small) dogs. They even come in all-terrain models with night reflectors for those Poodles who love fireside camp-outs but hate the hike to the lake (might chip the nail polish, of course). Will you be a little self-conscious walking your pup in a stroller? You can always just tell people that the gene for hairiness runs in your family!

Snugglies are another adaptation of a typical human-baby item, in this case a carrier. The dog is safely strapped into a front-pack or backpack with his head out and legs dangling, and then he's strapped onto his favorite human for a free ride. This is a good hands-free solution for long treks where the dog needs to be carried.

TOTE BAGS

Every pocket pooch needs a tote bag. It's the one must-have accessory, whether it's a $25 Louis Vuitton knock-off from a street

vendor (how gauche!) or a $700 Donald J. Pliner bag (worth every cent!). If you're like most pocket-pooch owners, you'll have more than one. Who wants to carry the same bag every day? One of the advantages to having a small dog is that you can sneak him in just about anywhere you go. This gives you a special bond with the dog that you wouldn't have otherwise—of course, it can also pave

the way to "incurably spoiled." One of the nicest aspects of having a pocket pooch is being able to travel easily with him. All you need is a safe bag or carrier and a few little essentials to make the trip safe and comfortable.

If you're traveling far from home, each airline has its own rules about pets flying with their owners. Since you have a pocket pooch, you can just bring him into the cabin in a safe carrier and put him under your seat. Do not put your little dog into the cargo hold. It's too dangerous and you'll do nothing during the flight but worry, cry and irritate the flight attendants. You'll have to pay an extra fee to bring your pet on board, but you won't have to wait for a certain time of year to fly; there are only embargo dates for pets going into the cargo space on the plane, not for those flying in the cabin. Tip: buy a pet travel bag with wheels; they are much easier to transport.

DOGGIE DUDS

Nobody likes ill-fitting couture, not even the most casual of canines. Imagine the sneers little Princess will get from the other Yorkies if her tilty tiara slips off when she's tinkling. She'll never regain her composure and could be scarred for years. Most pet boutiques will let your dog try garments on, but if you don't happen to have him with you at the shop, you'll have to know his measurements. The measurement you're primarily concerned with is the length in inches from the top of the dog's shoulders (base of the neck) to the base of his tail. Always measure the dog while he's standing. A measurement of 8 inches, for example, will correspond to clothing tags or packaging, which should indicate what size dog the garment will fit. Usually, XXS fits 4–6 inches, XS fits 7–9 inches and S fits 10–14 inches, but this depends largely on the manufacturer. The tag may also indicate that a garment will fit certain breeds, which you can use as a guideline. Except for the Pug and the English Toy Spaniel, most pocket pooches aren't barrel-chested, so you don't have to worry about measuring the dog around the chest.

Pocket pooches living in colder climates will do well with a wardrobe consisting of a couple of T-shirts, a sweater, a collared coat and a raincoat. Most raincoats come with a hood, but make sure

it's detachable, because some dogs don't like hoods or hats. Layer clothing when the weather is very cold. And don't forget the staple of any dog's wardrobe, the bandanna, which now comes in tiny-dog sizes.

Because your tot is so easily toted, he'll need some formal party wear. Sportswear just doesn't fly in the evening. Sure, *fur* is always sporty, but please don't embarrass Fritzy by forcing him to show up in his dog-day suit. For the evening, you can do anything from a hip rock-and-roll style to courtly wear, from the classic tux and taffeta gown to velvet and brocade. If it's stylin' in human fashion, it's stylin' in doggie fashion. Just keep a close eye on Boujee if you have her wearing anything bejeweled—you don't want her to swallow any of the bling.

FOOTWEAR

How fashionable can Fiona feel walking around bare-pawed? Let's not be crazy: you really can't buy Jimmy Chew (or Choo) pumps for your budding princess, even if you had that kind of cash. However, there may actually be a call for doggie footwear. Some dogs hate to get their feet wet. If Comet takes the long way around puddles, you know you've got a foot diva. Additionally, if you live in a place where there's salt and chemicals on the sidewalks during the snowy months, you'll need to equip your little dog with paw protection. For the correct sizing of shoes or boots, measure from the back edge of the big paw pad to the front edge of the middle small paw pad.

"These Boots Are Made for Walking" and put the booties on her for 20 or 30 seconds. If she doesn't fuss (she may not like *that* Sinatra), give her treats and praise, then take them off. If she objects to the whole process, you'll know that she has more sophisticated musical taste than you expected, but she may always have wet feet. If the exercise goes well, repeat it, leaving the boots on for longer periods of time until she walks normally with them. You can even get doggie socks to put over Baby's feet to keep the footwear from falling off and to make it more tolerable and comfortable.

Don't just spring boots on the dog at the first sign of a few flurries. The new sensation on Cinderella's feet might cause her to freeze in panic and she might not want to move an inch. She may also fight to get the shoes off or mince around awkwardly, even forgetting the main reason why she's on a walk. Instead, acclimate her to the boots when she's a puppy. Begin by doing your best Nancy Sinatra, hum a few bars of

HEAD WEAR

Do dogs love hats? If you love them, Bella will probably love them too. Dogs respond to their owners with an empathy that's beyond mind-reading, so if you're excited about her new Swarovski-adorned felt cowboy hat, well, doggone it, she will probably like it too (that is, if it's remotely comfortable).

A tiara is a must for any little doggie debutante with big hair. Most have a barrette in the back so you can attach it easily to dogs with longer hair. The look stands out on its own—no need for any outfit or other accessory. Don't let baby Edith become a fashion victim!

For eye protection from those nasty ultra-violet rays, try a pair of Doggles® tinted sunglasses for dogs. What's more *apropos* in the summer months than chic chapeaux, cool shades and sporty tennis shirts for both dog and owner?

DOG STAIRS

Is Sassy too small to jump on the bed? Get a set of portable dog stairs and park them at the foot of the bed. Sassy might need a little encouragement to learn to use the stairs, but just put her favorite treat on each step and she'll learn to climb them with ease. You can also find ramps and variously sized cubes that serve the same purpose. Many small dogs are injured badly by jumping off a high bed or couch; teacups are prone to breaking limbs from jumping off the bed. The repeated impact of landing can also damage ligaments and cartilage and cause early arthritis. Either lift Sassy in and out of bed or get her a set of stairs.

CAR SEAT AND HARNESS

Don't let Coco ride in the car without strapping her in safely. In the event of an accident, a body in motion will stay in motion, an unfortunate law of physics that can lead to broken bones or even more disastrous results. You can get a car booster seat made just for small dogs that allows Coco to look out the window and be strapped in at the same time. Or you can get a special dog harness that hooks up to your seat belt so Coco can be strapped securely to the seat. If you don't like these options, strap a hard carrier into the back seat with a seat belt and put Coco inside. Lastly, you can always let your pooch travel in his crate, which is the safest, if not the most stylish and fun, way of traveling with your pal.

Pocket Pooch Socialization

ocialization is the process of having your puppy experience lots of different people, other animals, new sounds and new objects while he's under 20 weeks old so that he's prepared to take those things in stride when he's an adult. The window for socialization is very short—from about 3 weeks to 16–20 weeks. After that, a puppy's opinions about the world have been formed, and it's more difficult to introduce the dog to new things without his being naturally apprehensive. The world is a big, busy place, and if you don't introduce the dog to most of it, he'll have a difficult time warming up to new people, new dogs and new situations. He may become fearful, socially inept and even aggressive. He may not understand how to interact with, play with or read the body language of other dogs or how to behave around children. Socialization has to happen when the puppy is young; it is not something you can do "next month" when you have more time or are on vacation.

Tiny dogs are often socialized poorly because their owners tend to coddle them or pick them up whenever they're feeling afraid, tentative or threatened. Poor behavior isn't innate in tiny dogs. Little dogs that are carried around constantly as puppies never learn to walk well on a leash and can

vinyl, wood, puddles and so on. Some puppies are afraid of smooth, slippery surfaces, which is a great excuse to sneak Prince Pickles into the mall—nothing more slippery than a polished marble floor. Reward him with praise and treats for confident steps onto a scary surface. Don't pick him up when he's afraid unless he really has something to be afraid of.

Puppies should be exposed to and allowed to play with other puppies and dogs, as long as all parties are properly vaccinated and everyone plays nicely. Puppy play dates are a great way to let your

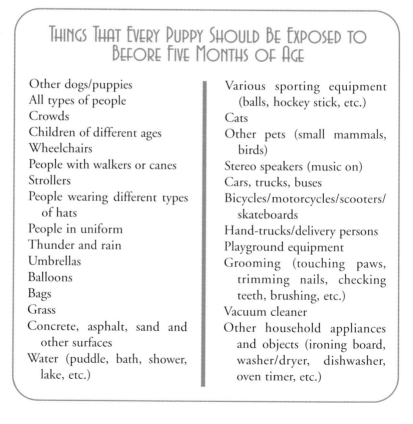

Things That Every Puppy Should Be Exposed to Before Five Months of Age

Other dogs/puppies
All types of people
Crowds
Children of different ages
Wheelchairs
People with walkers or canes
Strollers
People wearing different types of hats
People in uniform
Thunder and rain
Umbrellas
Balloons
Bags
Grass
Concrete, asphalt, sand and other surfaces
Water (puddle, bath, shower, lake, etc.)

Various sporting equipment (balls, hockey stick, etc.)
Cats
Other pets (small mammals, birds)
Stereo speakers (music on)
Cars, trucks, buses
Bicycles/motorcycles/scooters/skateboards
Hand-trucks/delivery persons
Playground equipment
Grooming (touching paws, trimming nails, checking teeth, brushing, etc.)
Vacuum cleaner
Other household appliances and objects (ironing board, washer/dryer, dishwasher, oven timer, etc.)

pup socialize and learn to properly interact with his fellow canines. When puppies don't interact with other puppies, they never learn social cues from other dogs, which can lead to fear- or dog-aggression as the dog grows into adulthood. Playing with other dogs should always be a fun experience, so the dogs should be well matched by age, energy level and/or size—don't let your pocket pooch get walloped by a bigger dog.

THE FEARFUL TYKE

Around 8 to 11 weeks, puppies go through what's known as the "fear imprint period"; this also happens again periodically between about 6 and 14 months of age. During these times a pup may lose some of his confidence and trust and become fearful of things and situations that he used to deal with easily. Anything that really traumatizes the pup during the fear imprint period can affect him for his entire life. Avoid unnecessary trips to the veterinarian or groomer, and make any big changes as comfortable as possible for the pup. Don't look at fear behavior as a setback. Just proceed with socialization in small incre-

ments. Rather than shoving a new object or person into the pup's environment, reward the puppy for just noticing the object.

When there's no real danger or threat, resist the urge to coddle and baby-talk to your puppy. For example, when it's thundering outside and Otis is shaking, cowering or showing fearful behavior, ignore it or try to start a game of

first and getting to do the wild thing first at canine orgies.

Depending on the pup's personality and how he behaved with his littermates, he may try to become dominant over everyone in the household or just over certain members, like the children or other pets. Many of the small terriers will try to become pack leader. Some pups will never challenge the pack order and will fall right into line if the humans in their pack behave in a way that they understand as leadership. Pups that challenge the pack order will need frequent reminders of their place in the pack. When training your puppy, you have to think like the "big, bossy wolf."

Remember that pack leaders are always human. All humans in the household are ahead of all dogs in the pack hierarchy. If there are various dogs in the household, they will work out their own pack hierarchy, but no dog should be allowed to challenge a human family member. Challenges include disobedience, mounting, growling, teeth-baring, refusal to move from a certain spot and food or toy guarding.

Who's Training Whom?

Your perfectly coiffed, incredibly cute pocket pup is too pretty to be smart and obedient. Little dogs don't have to be trained, they just have to look fabulous and attract a crowd. Don't believe this for a moment! Just because your little starlet is tiny and gorgeous doesn't mean that he doesn't need training. Even though you can pick him up and tuck him away when he's misbehaving, plotting or scheming, it doesn't make his behavior acceptable. You do not want to live with a manipulative pretty boy who never listens to you when you speak. That's what your boyfriend is for. Not only does your self-centered twerp ignore you when you speak, sometimes he even snaps at you ("but it doesn't *really* hurt"). Snap out of it before one of you ends up in a shelter. Six out of the list of the 18 dogs most apt to bite are pocket pooches. If Pekingese, Maltese and Mini Schnauzers weighed 100 pounds, they'd quickly be illegal to own!

Training is also essential for the dog's well-being. A small dog that knows to come when he's called and responds to basic commands is more likely to avoid dangerous situations. Before a snot-nosed pre-teen on a scooter or a psychotic Rottie can flatten your Pug, he flawlessly sit-stays his way out of harm. This chapter will give you some basic training to get you started.

DIPLOMA

the crate gradually and always in a positive manner.

During the day, place the crate in a room that you spend a lot of time in. You can move the crate into your bedroom at night. Make the crate comfortable with a washable fluffy crate mat, a cozy blanket and a few safe toys. Place some irresistible treat bits inside the crate and lure your pup with a treat to find them. Praise and treat any time he sets even a foot inside.

Next, show the irresistible food-stuffed toy to the pup and place it inside the crate. If he wants to spend some time in the crate, wonderful. If not, don't force him.

Treat and praise for any time he spends in the crate, but be sure not to praise him for coming out of the crate. You don't want him to think that leaving the crate is what he's supposed to do; you want him to become comfortable inside it. Repeat the aforementioned routine several times a day for a few minutes at a time.

At night, the pup will sleep in his crate with the door closed. At bedtime, lure him into the crate with a treat and have the peanut butter-filled toy inside to keep him distracted as he's settling in.

As he gets used to the crate, you will begin to up the ante. Wait

ANTICIPATION

If your pup whines during the night, place your hand near the crate and talk soothingly to him. Do not take him out! He'll learn that whining gets him a free ticket out of the crate, and you don't want to set this annoying, irreversible precedent. If the pup is very young and he starts getting genuinely restless, take him outside to relieve himself and praise him highly when he does. Never put him in the situation where he has to eliminate inside the crate. That means getting up from bed, the sofa, the Thigh Master anytime and every time you think the pup's signaling you to go potty. Anticipate the pup's elimination times—first thing in the morning, a few minutes after he eats and just before going to bed, for starters. Small-breed puppies need at least seven to eight elimination trips a day.

a little longer to give him the treat. Wait for him to go all the way inside the crate, then to go all the way in and turn around, then to go all the way in, turn around and remain in the crate for a few seconds, then for him to remain in the crate for a few seconds with the door closed. Remember to praise and treat while he is still in the crate, not as he is coming out. You are praising him for spending time inside the crate. Also, just as you would overnight, do not let him out if he starts whining and scratching; wait until he quiets down to give him a treat and praise and release him from the crate.

Keep practicing, increasing the amount of crate time. You will start to move across the room, then leave the room and then leave the house. When your dog's bladder is ready, you can be out of the house for a few hours.

Some people choose to house-train using an exercise pen or a small room, generally the kitchen or a bathroom, sectioned off with a baby gate. This is fine, but you should incorporate a crate into the area as well and do some crate training. The crate will be the dog's bed and safe haven. It's crucial to use the crate along with any other form of confinement so that your dog is used to the crate when you have to travel or when he needs to be kenneled. Small dogs are often paper-trained, so leaving him in an ex-pen or a gated-off room with a crate and some paper is fine.

Often the pup will seem to be doing great, settling down for longer and longer durations in the crate, and then have a setback. Just go back to the beginning. Make it fun. Treat, treat, treat! And remember not to abuse the crate.

Clicker training is a great positive-reinforcement technique and there are plenty of good books about it. It's easy, fun and highly effective. With this method, you concentrate on rewarding good behaviors and ignoring behaviors that you don't want (it's a little more complex, but that's the basic idea).

When the puppy does something you want, he'll get a reward; when he doesn't, he gets nothing at all. No eye contact, no saying his name, no physical contact. Eventually, the pup will realize that when he performs a certain behavior, he gets attention and a reward, but when he doesn't perform the asked-for behavior, he gets nothing. It's hard-wired into your puppy's brain to want your attention and rewards.

MY NAME IS FIDO

Beyond socialization and house-training, the most important thing to teach your dog is his name and to pay attention when you speak it. Always say your puppy's name in conjunction with something pleasant, like petting or treats. Never, *ever* use your pup's name when scolding him. Scolding by calling the pup's name or using the name along with a reprimand (like *no!*) will only result in the dog's becoming wary of responding to his name and can even cause him to ignore his name, which is the last thing you want.

Start using your puppy's name as soon as he's in your care. Realize that he doesn't know his name yet, so you can't expect him to respond when you say it. You have to teach him his name, and a clicker is great for that. Here I will explain a process for teaching pup his name and introduce the basics of clicker training, which you can use in teaching your dog anything.

Start in a small room that has few distractions. This is going to

be tough, because nearly every object and smell is interesting for a young puppy that's just getting to know his world. Do the best you can.

STEPS TO SUCCESS

You have to enforce every cue (command) that you give. This is why it's critical not to "name" a cue until you're sure that the puppy understands the behavior. If you're constantly asking for a "sit" and your pup ignores you, he will assume that it's okay to ignore you. Your puppy *must be successful* in his training or he won't learn, so you want to set him up for success. Only ask the puppy to do things that you're fairly certain he will do correctly. Train in small steps to elicit correct responses, click and treat often and don't hesitate to go back to an easier step if the pup gets distracted or isn't offering the behavior well anymore. Don't get frustrated when you have to backtrack—this is part of the training process.

Have your clicker handy. A clicker, in case you don't know, is a small plastic box, about the size of your thumb, with a button that makes a clicking noise when pressed and released. Click the clicker a few times, each time giving the puppy a treat so that he will start to understand that a click equals a treat and that it's time to pay attention. As the puppy explores the room, get his attention by making a sound, like patting your thigh, clapping softly or clucking your tongue. Just as he's turning his head, say his name excitedly—Elvis!—and then click and treat him. If he comes to you, even better.

Click and treat for any recognition of his name, even if it's just a half-turn of the head. Eventually, you will up the ante and will click/treat only for a full turn of the head when you say his name. Then, you will click/treat only when he turns his body toward you. Click and treat only on his recognizing and responding to his name. End the session on a good note, when the pup has responded to his name, and give him a few treats.

Most puppies will learn their names fairly easily. Avoid using nicknames until you're sure that your pup knows his actual name. Remember to praise when he recognizes his name, and never use his name in conjunction with anything he might consider unpleasant.

Don't overuse the puppy's name. The idea is to get his attention every time you say his name. If you're using it all the time in baby talk or repeating it like crazy to get his interest, he will learn to tune out his name and he won't come to it every time you call him. When you're talking about him to someone else, call him "the puppy" or "our dog."

Paying Attention

The first step to getting your pup to come to you reliably (the recall) is to make yourself the most exciting, best thing since champagne and strawberries and Paris. You have to get your pup's attention and keep it. Being at your side should be safe, pleasant and fun for him, but you have a lot of competition out there. Squirrels racing up trees, animal scents and that hunky mailman are all more exciting than you. So how are you going to compete with all that fluttering

and musk? This is a good job for the clicker and treats. Once your pup knows his name pretty reliably, you'll work on getting him to pay close attention to you (actually, you can do "name recognition" and "paying attention" basically simultaneously).

To practice and reinforce "pay attention," have your clicker and a small bag of treats on hand. Start in a room that has few distractions. "Prime" the clicker by clicking it and offering treats; this puts the clicker/treat association at the forefront of pup's mind and gets him motivated to earn more treats.

Call his name excitedly and click and treat when he responds. You can also say "Good boy!" Say the pup's name only once. If you call him too many times, the power of the name gets diluted and the pup may start to ignore you.

Next, just sit back and watch him carefully—do nothing. Anytime he looks at you, click and treat; be quick with your timing. If he gets too excited, end the session for a few minutes, then come back to it once he's distracted with something else.

Next, click and treat only for eye contact, even if just for a moment. Be quick with the click, because you don't want to reward for the moment he looks away. You may have to first lure his gaze to yours by putting the treat in between your fingers and holding it up, next to one of your eyes. When he looks at your eyes, click and treat. Next, stop luring and wait for him to look at you. You're better off waiting than to keep luring, so keep those treats hidden until he looks.

Move your practice outside with your pup on leash. Let him explore anything at the end of the leash, and click and treat when he pays any attention to you or moves toward you (even if it's not eye contact). You are rewarding him for staying close to you and paying attention to you around distractions. Progress to clicking/ treating only for eye contact, even if just for a split second. Then up the ante by waiting for a full second, two seconds, etc. Be generous with the treats; don't rush or expect too much.

As he becomes reliable with making eye contact on leash, you will then progress to having pup on a long line and then to letting him off leash in a fenced-in area, repeating the process as described.

If you get good at carrying a clicker all of the time during the training process, you can click and praise when your pup comes to find you when you're just watching television or reading a book—use these moments as training opportunities. If you don't have the clicker handy, try to approximate the sound of the clicker by clucking your tongue twice and then praising.

Don't be fooled by the young puppy that likes to be near you and always comes when called. This same dog can do a turnaround when he hits adolescence. Test and reinforce eye contact around a lot of distractions, and keep returning to this basic behavior to keep it conditioned.

THE RECALL

The recall (*come!*) is the most important cue (command) that you'll ever teach your dog. Your dog should come to you every time you call, without fail, no matter what. It doesn't matter how great Sassy feels when she's chasing that bicycle or digging under the fence. When you call, your dog should stop what she's doing and come to

you. In a perfect world, this would happen all the time. But some breeds are known to get very distracted in certain situations; for example, terriers are intent on chasing small animals. The goal is for an owner to make coming to him the most exciting thing ever so that his dog will want to give up whatever he is doing to come to his owner's side.

The recall is the most fun cue to teach because it's rewarding for both dog and owner. Every time you call the dog to you, there has to be a pleasant reward for him when he reaches you. Yes, you have to praise him even if he has just spent an hour running away from you. When he comes back, *it's always good.*

You can reinforce the recall with a game. Find another person to help you; this game is particularly fun for kids. Start by priming the clicker as previously mentioned. You and your helper will sit down on opposite sides of a room; take turns calling the puppy by name and click/treat upon his arrival (as he reaches you, but before he touches you).

If you click too late, you may be reinforcing the wrong behavior,

like jumping up or licking, which can confuse the pup. Encourage the puppy as he's running to you—"Good boy! Yay!"

When puppy gets good at the game, repeat it with you and your helper standing up. Then progress to playing the game outside, first sitting and then standing, with the pup on his long line. When you're sure that the puppy understands that coming to you and the other person is what's expected of him,

begin to use the cue word "come." Say it firmly and with excitement. You can use the pup's name, too: "Sally, *come!*"

When Ozzie is very good at coming when called, take him on the long line to a busy place, like a park, and begin to test the recall. Don't rush taking him to a distracting place—make sure that the recall is conditioned well before you test it. If you rush things, you can undo what you've accomplished.

133

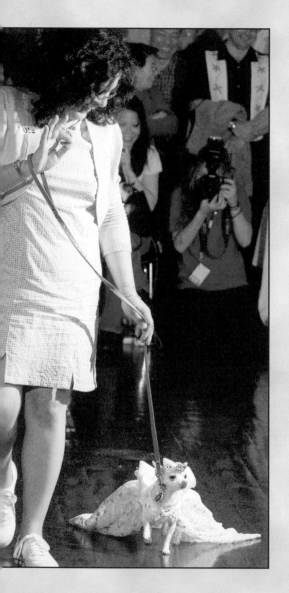

Use everyday situations to teach the recall, such as at mealtimes or when going outside, things that your dog likes. Eventually, you won't have to have a treat in your hand to get the pup to come to you. Try putting a treat across the room, calling the pup and then running over to the treat to get it and give it to him. Did he follow you? If so, he gets the treat.

Many dogs begin to associate the recall command with being captured or locked up. If the dog loses his freedom every time you call him, of course he's going to be wary of coming to you. Imagine that every time you shopped, they took your credit card away. You'd get pretty spooked about going to Bloomies again, wouldn't you? When Pepper is pretty reliable with the recall, call him to you, click/treat, and then let him go again. He'll realize that coming to you doesn't mean that it's time to leave the dog park.

Follow

After you've got a good recall going, start teaching your puppy to follow you. Start encouraging following behavior as soon as it starts. Use the clicker to reward random following whenever your pup does it on his own. When he's good at the recall, ask him to follow you into other rooms and around the fenced yard. Click and treat when he's following well, and then click and treat only when he's following right at your heels or at your side, but not ahead of you. If you have a wanderer on your hands, use a long line so that you can reel him in if you need to get his attention.

Up the ante again so that you click only when he's at your left side, either just behind you or at your side. Up the ante once more so that he gets rewarded only when he's at your side. If you have trouble getting him there, you can use a lure, but try to phase that out quickly. Click and treat often as he follows, but make sure not to stop as you do it—click on the move.

If you can get your pup to do all of this, you're at the first stages of teaching him to walk *with* you, not beyond you or behind you. Some people never teach their dogs to formally heel, but it's nice to condition this "informal heel" so that your dog will not only follow you but also will eventually walk nicely on a loose leash.

SIT

After the recall command, "sit" is the next most important cue to teach your pup. A reliable sit will not only turn your pup into a well-mannered individual that's pleasant to be around but also it can save his life someday. If Yogi has a reliable sit conditioned into him, you can call him out of danger and use the sit command as a backup. It also is important for your dog to sit politely to greet people and other dogs.

Teaching a dog to sit is the equivalent of teaching a child to say "please." Your pup should learn to sit before each meal, at the door before going out for a walk and at each curb before you cross the street. He should also sit on cue before playtime and when you need him to be calm.

Start teaching the sit by priming the clicker and standing up straight to show your authority. If you're dealing with a very small dog, then you can be on your knees or sitting in a chair. Have the pup in front of you, facing you. If he's a wanderer and it's difficult to get his attention, put him on a short leash. Don't pull and yank him—just keep him in front of you.

Show the dog that you have a treat in between your fingers. Hold it out so that it's just above his nose and then move it slowly back, toward his tail. Ideally, he should follow the treat with his eyes and, as his head goes back, his little butt should hit the ground. Ignore any missteps; you will react when the pup does something right, not when he does something wrong.

Click and treat for a sit, preferably clicking as the behavior is in the process of happening, just before his behind hits the ground. If your pup isn't offering a sit right away, start shaping the behavior in small increments. Click for any movement of the dog's butt toward the ground, no matter how small. Then up the ante, asking for the butt to go down further and further, until you're getting a real sit. When he starts sitting on his own in anticipation, it's time to start adding the cue word "sit." When you can get the pup to perform a few times without the clicker, then you know the cue has stuck.

On a side note: be careful of clicking too soon when you're training a short dog with short legs. It can be difficult to see if a little dog is actually sitting, especially if he's fluffy. You may have to lean to the side to make sure that his butt is really on the floor. Ah, the joys of pocket pooches!

THE RELEASE CUE

Once your dog knows how to sit very well, you'll start using a "release cue" to release the dog from the behavior (you'll also use

Just before he gets up from the sit on his own (watch for the smallest movement toward getting up), say "okay!" briskly and then click and treat. "Okay" is the only cue word that you will introduce from the get-go; with other commands, you teach the behavior and wait until the dog offers it before pairing it with a cue word.

Soon the pup will understand that he's being rewarded for getting up. He's also hearing your release word at the same time. Wait until the puppy is offering the getting-up behavior in anticipation of a treat. Ask for a sit again and make eye contact. See if you can get the pup to sit for half a second longer than usual. Say "okay!" and then click and treat.

As you progress, you'll want to click and treat for "sit" to keep reinforcing it as well as for "okay" when the dog gets up. If he gets up before you've released him, just wait dispassionately until he sits again and then looks up at you for direction. If you haven't been rushing it, this should happen. Otherwise, go back to more repetitions.

this release cue for "down," "stay" and "wait"). Buster should not think that it's okay to just get up from your commands whenever he wants.

The release cue I use is "okay." You can use another word, but "okay" doesn't sound like any other cue and it's a positive word, which is why I like it. You can also use "free," "go play" or another word, but choose just one.

To teach the release, first prime the clicker. Ask the puppy to sit and praise him verbally when he does it ("good boy!").

DOWN

"Down" isn't the easiest behavior to teach, but it's important. It can calm an excited puppy and prevents jumping and aggression. The down exercise can be tricky for some pups because it's a very submissive behavior, and many puppies aren't thrilled about being put into this position. However, if you continue to make training fun, then you shouldn't have trouble teaching the down command.

One way to teach the down is to ask the puppy to sit in front of you, place a treat near his nose (but don't let him grab for it) and then drop your hand in between his paws and pull it slowly away from him, along the floor. Ideally, his paws should slide forward and his elbows should touch the ground. Click and treat before he pops up from the down position. Once he is doing this well, practice the same way, but without a treat in your hand. Click and treat once he is in position.

Once he has offered the behavior a few times, withhold the click/treat until he lies down from a standing position instead of a sit. When he's offering the behavior freely, add the cue word "down."

If you aren't having any success with the aforementioned method, here's another one that doesn't follow the principles of clicker training, but is effective. Start with your puppy in the sitting position and crouch in front of him. Clasp one paw gently in each of your hands and slide his paws forward until the pup's elbows touch the ground. Give the pup a treat for being in the down position; repeat this a few times.

You can then bring out the clicker and wait for the pup to offer the down behavior. If he doesn't, put him in a sit and try to lure him down, but don't pull his paws this time. Treat him for being lured down, then wait again for him to offer the behavior. He will probably try some different behaviors to see what it is that gets him the reward.

LEASH TRAINING

Puppies don't naturally know how to walk nicely on a leash down Park Avenue (or even down a dirt road). It's in a puppy's nature to want to pull to get to where he wants to go, and that might not be where *you* want to go. While

ing just ahead, like an animal to chase, another dog or a scent. Some little dogs get frightened easily and will put on the brakes and refuse to go any farther. Usually, this is about the time that the owner picks Titan up and carries him the rest of the way. If you carry your pup everywhere, or if you let him pull sometimes when you're in a hurry but then try to train him not to pull at other times, you're just going to have a confused puppy. You have to commit to consistent loose-leash training.

Start by attaching the leash to the pup's harness; you will hold the leash and clicker in your left hand and the treats in your right hand. Stand still. The pup will probably walk to the end of the leash, making it taut. Ignore him until he releases the tension in the leash, even for a fraction of a second. The instant he releases the tension, click and treat.

Next, walk a few steps and follow the same procedure: click and treat the second that the pup lets the leash go slightly slack. Do this a few times. Then, when the pup pulls one way, turn and walk the other way. When he follows,

it's very tempting to carry your little dog everywhere, this doesn't do much to help him learn to walk nicely on the leash. Ideally, your pup should walk on a loose leash. You don't have to enforce a strict "heel" unless you're doing obedience.

Some pups are very stubborn when it comes to walking nicely—there's always something interest-

click and treat. Don't pull or yank. Just walk and click and treat for any behavior that you like.

Every time the puppy pulls, and I mean *every time*, you will stop and wait for the leash to slacken, at which point you will click and treat. If you have a chronic puller, you may not get very far on the first few walks. That's okay—have patience and just keep trying.

Make leash training fun. Coax and lure Nanette if you have to in the beginning (pups who won't budge will especially need to be lured), and remember to praise like crazy when she walks nicely, even for a second. Eventually she'll get the idea that she's only going somewhere when the leash is loose and she's walking with some composure. Treat, treat, treat!

When you've got the pup walking decently on a loose leash, you can begin adding the cue "let's go!" Make it a happy cue, not a forceful one.

STAY

The stay command is very important for a pup's safety. "Stay" is an odd command for a pup. What's he supposed to actually *do*? Much of clicker training relies on "muscle memory," but there is no muscle action for the body to remember with the stay command. Like all of

the other commands, this one takes patience and an abundance of praise and treats.

The key to teaching "stay" is taking it very slowly and allowing your dog to learn in very small increments. You will be rewarding for a fraction-of-a-second stay, then a one-second stay, then two seconds and so on, until your dog will sit/stay or down/stay for ten minutes. But we're getting ahead of ourselves. Let's start at the beginning.

Put a leash on your pup's harness and hold it firmly about three inches away from the end closest to the dog. Kneel down next to your pup and have him sit; when he sits, place a treat just out of his reach. When he goes for it, hold his collar firmly and put him back into the sit (don't treat for this second sit). The second he relaxes, click and give him the treat. You are looking for the tiny moment that he backs off from wanting to lunge at the treat.

Repeat the drill for "stay" until the dog understands the game. The idea is to get him to relax in the sit for just a moment, then for a second, then two seconds and so on. Don't rush. Take it slowly until the dog really understands.

When it's clear that your pup gets what's going on, stand in front of him with your foot holding down the leash and ask him for a sit. Hold your palm up and flat a couple of feet away from his face (as if you're motioning for someone to stop) and then drop a treat in front of him, but far enough away that he can't snatch it. Your foot is on the leash, so he's not going to get far. Put him back in a sit and repeat until he relaxes, then click/treat. Give him your release command ("okay") and praise him. Treat only for the stay at this stage, not for his getting up at the release command. Once he seems to understand the game, add the cue word "stay" when you hold up your palm.

Work on this in small increments—reward for one second, then two, then three and so on. When you can get up to 60 seconds, start varying the amount of time that you require him to stay. Allow him to get up only when you give the release command. If he gets up, put him back into the sit/stay. Remember that one of the keys to teaching your dog to stay is to avoid reinforcing the release command, so don't treat when the dog gets up, only when he is sitting.

You will then progress to working on a loose leash, and then on a long line, gradually increasing your distance from the dog. You can backtrack at any time that you need to.

You will eventually work up to moving 10 feet away from the dog, then 20, then 50 and so on. Eventually, you will also work on getting the dog to stay when you are out of sight, such as somewhere else in the house for a few minutes. Work on this very slowly, increasing the criteria in small increments and being generous with rewards. The fundamental principle of clicker training is that the dog must be successful every time.

Once you have a good sit/stay, begin teaching down/stay using the same protocol. Finally, begin to "proof" or test the stay exercise by offering distractions. Roll a ball by the dog, show him his favorite toy, drop a treat. The idea is not to trick him into breaking the stay, but rather to reward him for the one or two seconds he does stay even though there's a ball nearby. Then move on to distractions outdoors in an enclosed area. Just because Pepper stays nicely for five minutes in the living room doesn't mean he'll stay for even a second when he sees a squirrel. You have to work on making him understand that obeying your stay command is much more rewarding than chasing that squirrel. Make it fun and don't skimp on the treats!

WAIT

"Wait" is a great cue and it's not as tough to teach as the stay command. I think this might be because you're asking the dog to just pause for a moment before he gets to do something he wants, like go through a doorway, take a toy or eat.

To teach "wait," put the pup on a leash as if you're going out for a walk. No doubt that Fifi will be excited and want to rush out the door. Well, she's got a surprise coming! You'll be holding her back with the leash.

Choose a spot that will be the dog's "threshold" to wait behind before going outside. For example, you can use a doormat at his threshold or even put down a length of duct tape. The tape is good because once he learns to stand behind it, you can use it anywhere you want to get the same behavior.

Walk the pup to the door and stop him just a few inches before the tape; don't let him go beyond. Wait for him to understand that he's not going any farther and then for him to either back off or sit down, at which point you click and treat. Repeat this until he begins pausing on his own at the tape and then looking up at you for his treat—now he understands the game. Add the cue word "wait," but instead of saying it firmly, the way you'd say "sit" or "down," say it slow and in a low tone: "waaaaiiiiit."

Next, open the door just a little, and click/treat when he waits. Then practice opening it further as he waits. Remember to always let him be successful in his training and not to push for big results too soon. One short training session before each of your walks should do the trick.

144

If he insists on breaking his threshold as you reach for the doorknob, say "sorry" and go back to your original starting point. He must understand that he's not getting treats or going anywhere unless he waits.

Reinforce the wait command at mealtime or when offering toys or treats. Practice "wait" before allowing the pup to get into the car, before coming into the house (he might have muddy paws that need to be wiped off) and before getting on the furniture.

SHAKE A PAW

This is an easy trick that most dogs will pick up in a matter of minutes. With your dog sitting, kneel in front of him. Press your index finger gently but firmly into the top of his right paw. When he lifts his paw slightly because it's kind of uncomfortable, click and treat. Repeat this step until he's lifting his paw a little more. Raise your criterion and click and treat for higher lifts. Once he is lifting his paw higher, knowing you'll click for that, take the paw briefly and gently in your hand and shake it—click and treat. When he has the hang of this game, add the cue word "shake"

or "foot." You can then teach him to shake his other paw.

If your dog loves shaking a paw, and most dogs do, you can start training the "high five" by asking for a shake and then holding your hand up in a high-five position, adding the cue "high five" when he understands that this is different from the shake. You will be rejecting a low shake and accepting only a high five. You can then turn that into a "wave" by asking for a high five and pulling your hand back slightly as he raises his paw. Up the ante in small increments until the dog is waving his paw a couple of times in the air.

8

Pocket Pooch Problem Behaviors

Rules aren't just for chumps. All dogs, from the 100-pounders to the wee McDogs you can put into a paper sack, need to know how to behave. Puppies don't understand the house rules when they first come home. Even a puppy that has been taught some rules will have lapses. But puppyhood doesn't have to be filled with a series of small tragedies. Proper supervision and training will help Pandora from opening up her box of bad behavior.

BARKING

It's not for no reason that many small dogs are known as yappers. "Put a cork in it" might be a phrase you know only from your wine-tasting trips in Sonoma, but Mini Schnauzer owners use it every day. Some little dogs bark because they are reacting to something, while some bark out of boredom and habit. Others bark incessantly because of separation anxiety. It's difficult to break the barking pattern of a reactive barker, especially if everything makes him bark—the postman, bicycles, squirrels, noises, other dogs going by and so on. The best solution for this type of dog is heavy socialization. Get him used to the things he barks at so that they become commonplace.

Reactive barkers tend to go nuts when the doorbell rings or someone knocks. When a visitor comes over, a barking dog may scare her at the door, not to mention embarrass you. If your puppy is starting to react to strangers at the door, here is a training protocol to discourage this behavior.

Keep a container of great treats at the door along with your clicker. Have a friend help you by coming over and knocking on the door. When the dog goes nuts, show him the treat and shove it into his mouth the second he stops barking. Click at the same time if you're quick enough (though in this case everything happens so quickly that you can use just the treat). The idea here is that you're treating for the behavior of stopping barking, not for running to the door and barking, so make sure that your timing is right and you're treating for the correct behavior.

The next step is to put a mat or bed close to the door and have your friend knock again. Lure the pup to the mat and give him the treat when he complies. Next, lure him to the mat and ask for a sit. Click and treat. Remember that this

kind of training can take weeks, even months, so don't rush it.

When someone knocks at the door, the dog is allowed a few warning woofs, but then he should automatically go to his mat by the door and sit or lie down and be quiet. He can even stand there if that's okay with you, but he's got to stand there quietly. He should be conditioned to expect a treat for this, so give it to him. That's what the treat jar at the door is for. Remember to reward for very small increments of success. Don't expect a miracle. Just keep working on it and remember to treat, treat, treat! This is one of the most difficult behaviors to break, so just reward for little breakthroughs and you should come out on top.

Of course, dogs react to many things in addition to someone at the door, so you'll have to work on them one by one as they arise. It's natural for dogs to react vocally; many are just "doing their job" by sounding the alarm, but you want to keep his barking under control. The key is to be precise with your timing so that the dog is being rewarded for being quiet, not for barking. You can use the word "quiet" as you hand over the treat so that eventually the command alone

will suffice to quiet him after a few woofs.

Boredom barkers and those dogs barking because of separation anxiety need something to do with their energies. Long-lasting chew treats and food-filled toys help, as does keeping the television on while you're gone. Exercise also helps bored or anxious dogs because it allows them to expend some of the energy that they would otherwise be using to bark, dig, chew, tear up your sofa, etc.

NIPPING AND MOUTHING

Peppermint might be the cutest Maltese puppy *ever-wever yes you are*, but when she puts her little teeth into your skin, she's not so adorable anymore. Puppies nip when they play, especially when they become overstimulated. When the puppy was still with his littermates, his mother reprimanded him with a growl or yip when he nipped, or even by getting up and leaving. His littermates squealed in pain from a nip, which told the pup that he was biting too hard. So if you want to speak your puppy's language, you have two options—yelp or leave.

When the puppy nips during play or when taking a treat too vigorously (when you can feel teeth), you will yelp "ow!" to let the pup know that he has "hurt"

you. I guarantee that if you're giving it your best Academy Award-winning performance, he will stop in his tracks. When he does, you click and treat. You are treating for him stopping the behavior, not for nipping. Then, thank the Academy.

If he nips as he's taking food from your hand, practice the command "gentle" by holding the food tightly in your hand, just hidden enough so that he can still see and smell it, and then yelp and retract your hand and the food when you feel teeth. Then, offer the food to him again and say "gentle" in a low tone, dragging the word out slowly. If you feel teeth again, pull back again and yelp. Repeat this a few times and your pup will learn to take treats without taking your fingers with them. He gets the treat only when he's gentle.

If the nipping is incessant, get up, turn your back on the pup and stop the game. He doesn't get to play if he's not going to behave. It's like dating. If he's not going to open the car door, you're certainly not going to get in. Once the pup stops nipping, turn back to him and begin interacting with him

again, yelping when he nips and getting up and ignoring him for a moment. If he nips at your ankles, give him something else to chew on, like a nice bone or chew toy, and then put him into his crate until he can calm down. You are not punishing him or scolding him—this is just a "time out" that allows him to gather himself before the next play session.

Anytime you feel puppy teeth on your skin, you need to either correct the behavior or refocus it. Try smearing the tops of your hands with peanut butter (a very light coating) and have your puppy lick it off. Praise and treat for licking—this shows the puppy that kisses get rewards, but bites do not.

CHEWING

Puppies like to chew things because it's their way of exploring the world and because they are teething, and, like babies, they have to put everything into their mouths. Chewing is a natural behavior, but it needs to be directed toward acceptable objects, like hard rubber toys, rope toys and other chew items made for dogs. The best way to save your home and furniture from a teething puppy is to not allow the puppy access to your things. Do not give him old socks and shoes to chew or he will think that he has *carte blanche* to sink his teeth into all footwear and won't understand why you're upset that he chewed your Prada pumps. Buy toys that you can fill with water and freeze to help with the pup's teething pain.

AGGRESSION

Wee wittle doggies can be as aggressive as those police dogs you see on television taking down a suspect on *COPS*, but with far less self-control. Aggression in small dogs is often seen as cute or funny. It's hilarious when Xena the Chihuahua attacks someone's sneaker (especially if it's a cheap no-brand sneaker) or guards her food, but the same behavior in a German Shepherd would be taken very seriously. If it's bad in one dog, why is it okay for a little dog? The answer is that *it's not*.

Some dogs display aggression toward humans, dog-on-dog aggression, or both. Your pup might show outright aggression only to kids or men, or perhaps only to bigger dogs. Most aggression stems from fear, generally due to a learned response. For example, a puppy may have been terrorized by a child and has learned to behave aggressively toward all children. Or the pup hasn't been exposed to many types of humans or other dogs and has become fearful of new encounters. Little dogs are especially susceptible to fearful aggression because they're always being pawed at and picked up by strangers.

There's a difference between real aggression and self-defense. Real aggression is when the dog launches an attack without being prompted, or perhaps with just the slightest cue. This kind of aggression should absolutely be trained out of a dog, which is not always easy. However, dogs have their own "language" and should be allowed to use it on each other when necessary. For example, if you're in the dog park and another dog is trying to mount your pup, he has every right to growl, show teeth, raise his hackles and bark a warning. This is to tell the other dog that the behavior is unacceptable. This is not

aggression. The first dog is behaving rudely and your dog is telling him so. Watch the two dogs carefully to make sure that the self-defense tactics don't escalate. This situation can turn into a downright fight if the mounting dog persists. If Humpy won't leave Fifi alone, the two dogs should be separated and the other owner informed of her dog's persistence. Remember that not every dog has to be friends with every other dog. You probably don't like

everyone in your neighborhood, so your dog doesn't have to either.

A dog that's defending himself hasn't done anything wrong, and you shouldn't work to quash behaviors that are not only innate in your pup, but are completely normal. Remember that you, as the puppy's human friend, are responsible for caring for your pup and keeping him safe. If you don't do anything to defend him, he will assume that he's alone in the situation, and his reaction might esca-

late. If another dog is bullying him, step into the situation and let him know that you're there. Don't coddle him or run to his side every time another dog is bothering him, but just be nearby so that he knows his pack leader is there just in case he really needs you. Little dogs can get hurt by larger dogs, and some larger dogs will even kill a small dog, so do defend your dog when it's necessary.

If your dog is exhibiting fearful or very submissive body language, such as a tucked tail, rolling over, yelping and urinating on himself, perhaps there's a valid reason for him to be afraid; maybe the dog that's bothering him hurt him when you weren't looking. Don't just let him "tough it out." Step in and remove him from the situation. Dogs do this for other dogs, so your pup will perceive it as normal behavior for his pack leader to defend him. So, remembering that your dog is very small and can be killed by a bigger dog, do not hesitate to help him if a bigger dog is hounding him.

Little dogs are prone to biting because they are constantly grabbed at and picked up by strangers. Rarely will a stranger come barreling up to a Pit Bull and start pawing at him, but a Chihuahua or Yorkie looks much more harmless. Who can blame a little dog that bites out of self-defense? It's up to you to prevent that from happening. Seventy percent of dog-bite victims are children.

Allowing aggressive or possessive behavior to continue will also result in biting, so you have to get it under control as soon as it starts. A truly aggressive

dog is a danger to society and a nuisance to himself and has to be dealt with immediately, even if he's three pounds soaking wet. If you feel that you can't deal with aggression on your own, please consult a trainer in your area who has experience in dealing with aggression issues in your breed.

RESOURCE GUARDING

Resource guarding is when a dog becomes possessive of something considered a "resource," usually food, a bone or a toy, but a dog will sometimes also guard a location, like his bed or a piece of furniture. This is actually normal, innate canine behavior, but it is not good manners in a household. This is where the wild meets the domestic and battles it out. The puppy feels compelled to guard his items, but that is unacceptable. This is the ultimate mixed message—one that comes from his instincts and the other that comes from his human leaders.

Instead of punishing a puppy for doing what comes naturally to him, you will condition the puppy to view any approaching family member as a benefit to him, not a threat. Every time a family member approaches him, something should be added to his life rather than taken away. For example, an approaching human should always have a treat or toy for the pup. Every time someone gives anything to the puppy—food, water, treat, toy—he should sit before he gets it. This should happen whether or not the puppy is prone to resource guarding.

For a pup that's guarding his food bowl, separate each meal into several small portions. Place each portion into the bowl and have him eat it while you're holding the bowl. Praise him as he eats. When he seems comfortable with this, start putting the food in the bowl and putting the bowl on the floor, then picking it up to add more food.

If the dog is still guarding his food bowl, approach the bowl with something even better, like a piece of boiled liver or a slice of hotdog—something more valuable than his regular food. Drop the treat into his dish and retreat. As the days go by, bring the hand with the treat closer and closer to the bowl. The idea is for the pup to understand that when you're near the bowl, he's going to get some-

thing better than what he already has. Eventually, you should be able to take food out of the bowl or remove the bowl without a growl. Have the whole family participate in this drill (supervise the kids), approaching the dog from all sides.

The next step is to be able to pet the dog and even take away a half-full food bowl while he's still eating. Start by adding something yummy to the bowl, then touching the pup lightly on the back. Continue in small steps until you can pet the dog as he eats. You will eventually be able to put your hand inside the food bowl as he eats, and even take the bowl away. Offer a treat as you take it away, and then ask him to sit to get the bowl back. Starting these drills when the pup is young will help avoid resource-guarding issues.

If your adolescent puppy already has resource-guarding issues, perhaps from being in a shelter with other dogs, take this training in very small increments and never push the pup beyond his comfort level. If you hear a growl, you've gotten too close. Back off and repeat the drill from a distance.

Always replace anything you've taken away with something

more valuable, something he would want more. If you want to take a bone away from the dog, approach him with something better, like a hot dog slice or a rubber toy stuffed with peanut butter and kibble. When he drops the bone to deal with the new item, you remove the bone. The idea is that when you approach, the dog will always know that something good is about to happen. If you're doing this as a drill, offer him the treat, take away the bone and then give him the bone again...and repeat.

Once the dog understands that you have something more valuable than he has, he will begin dropping the item that he has as soon as you approach in anticipation of the better thing. This is when you start using the cue "give it" as you take the other item away. When he has gobbled up the treat, give him the original item again and then ask him to "give it" back to you. If he drops the item, he gets the treat. Again, work in small increments to get this behavior, and backtrack if necessary. The "give it" cue is important to teach, especially if you walk your dog in urban areas where he can pick up

If the pup begins guarding his bed, his crate or a piece of furniture, begin training him out of this by asking him to come to the offending area by showing him that you have a treat. Lure him off or out of the area with the treat and then click/treat when he complies. Praise him and then ask him to come back into the area. Again, lure him off or away and click/treat and praise. Don't give the treat until all four feet are on the floor, off the dog bed, out of the crate, etc., and don't treat for coming up on or into the area, just for getting down or moving away. When he starts to understand the game, add the cue "off." If he still persists in growling when someone gets near his bed, move it to another spot or remove it altogether. If it's a couch or chair he's guarding, use a baby gate to prevent him from going into that area for a while.

Never punish a dog for having something of yours that you need back, like your sneaker. Imagine that you're a puppy and every time you have something good in your mouth, your human scolds you and takes it away. Well, not only would you probably hide

dangerous things off the street or in rural areas where he can find dead animals, which can carry parasites and germs or may have been poisoned.

FINDING A DOG TRAINER

Puppy kindergarten is a great idea for any puppy, and most dog-training schools will have classes just for small-breed dogs. You can also get one-on-one lessons from a trainer who has experience with small dogs. Make sure that the trainer uses only positive reinforcement and be sure to voice your concerns if the trainer does anything to your dog that you consider questionable. Find a trainer in your area at the Association of Pet Dog Trainers' website, www.apdt.com.

with your tasty item, you'd probably not want to drop it either. If you're consistent about offering something better in exchange for the thing you want, your pup won't have any reason to hide or hang onto the item he has.

If all else fails and the puppy is still guarding a certain object or place, remove it until he learns not to guard other things.

RUNNING AWAY

Puppies love a good game of chase. A solid recall proofed around distractions and a good sense of Puppy Psychology 101 is all you need to avoid having your pup run from you. There are a few things you can do to get your pup to come back to you when he's running away (before he has

learned a solid recall). One or more of these may work:

- Run the other way while saying his name excitedly. This changes the direction of the chasing game—now he's "it" and has to catch you!
- Stop in your tracks and become extremely excited about something happening on the ground right in front of you. Gasp, squeal, scream with joy—anything to get your pup to become interested and come back.
- Squeak the heck out of the squeaky toy to get the pup's attention, and then show him your bag of treats. If he doesn't come running, there must be a mighty fine squirrel on the other end of his chase.

Health and Feeding

Most small breeds have congenital issues or are prone to injuries of the legs and eyes, so it's important to know the signs of illness and injury in your particular breed. Do some research on your breed and the illnesses he's prone to and keep a list of the symptoms handy in case Kewpie starts to show signs of not feeling well. You can't diagnose your dog yourself, but you can go to the veterinarian with a few ideas of what you think the problem is (some vets dislike this, but you're the owner, so it's your right to ask questions and share information).

VACCINATIONS

Dogs are required to get a yearly rabies vaccine (or every three years in some states). They should also get the distemper and parvovirus vaccines, along with vaccines to protect against coronavirus, parainfluenza, hepatitis, *Bordetella* and Lyme disease based on the veterinarian's advice. Ask your veterinarian if he regularly vaccinates small dogs and if the whole dose is used on a very tiny dog. Also, inquire about possible negative reactions to vaccines. Some dogs have mild fever and aches after vaccines, and some can have more severe allergic reactions. Vaccines are started at 7 weeks, with boosters and

prevent her/him from having puppies. Breeding dogs is best left up to the experts. Small dogs are especially difficult to breed and can die while whelping, and puppy mortality is greater in small dogs than in bigger dogs. "Fixing" your dog actually helps him or her to live a longer and happier life by preventing or reducing the risk of certain cancers and other health problems. Speak with your veterinarian about the procedure and when he recommends performing it. For males, it's a relatively easy and quick procedure with fast healing time. For females, it's major surgery but still a fairly routine procedure.

PARASITES

Parasites such as worms, fleas and ticks can plague any dog, even your little tyke. Did you know that during the Victorian period, lap dogs were favored by ladies as flea "barriers"—the fleas went on the dogs, not the ladies! Today's pocket pooches aren't so selfless and don't like to be itchy any more than we do. There are many signs of parasitic infestation—get ready to be grossed out by this list: skin rash, sores, pustules, skin odor, ear odor,

additional vaccines given up to 16 weeks. Do not walk your dog around the neighborhood or put him down where any other dogs have been until he has completed his round of vaccines; ask your vet about timing for safe socialization and public outings.

SPAY/NEUTER

Unless you are an experienced breeder, please have your dog spayed or neutered, which will

itching, patchy fur, vomiting, diarrhea, bloating, coughing and the list goes on. Bugs are never a good thing! If you notice that your dog is behaving oddly or having any sort of itching or discomfort, get him to the veterinarian immediately. Use a flea preventive to keep the pests off him, but make sure to use a dosage appropriate to his small size. Also ask your vet about preventives for internal parasites; a heartworm preventive often protects your dog from other common parasites too.

EXERCISE

You haven't selected a portable Pap, Peke or Pom because you're looking for a jogging partner, so don't panic—you don't need to join Curves with your pooch or start taking cardio kickboxing classes together. Nevertheless, a certain amount of physical activity is critical to the health of even a teacup pooch, and fortunately most small dogs can get enough of it by playing in the house and going on moderate walks (without the stroller!). Porky dogs don't live as long as slim, fit dogs, so if you really love your petite pooch, keep him on the lean side. Some of the small terriers do need a lot more exercise than other small dogs, so find out what's best for your breed. Remember that the brachycephalic breeds (smush-faced dogs) can get heat stroke very easily, so keep them cool and don't overdo it in extreme temperatures. Also, some small dogs get cold very easily and need to always be dressed when outside in the winter.

FIFI'S FEAST

Small dogs (well, all dogs) should be fed a premium food. You may not be able to find this type of food at a regular pet-supply shop—you need a major pet supermarket or a "boutique"-type shop that carries a good selection of premium foods. Join an online forum about your breed and contact the breed's parent club to find out what other people are feeding your type of dog.

Fifi should get a combination of dry and wet food in order to keep her teeth clean and keep her interested in eating. A lot of small dogs are very fussy eaters, and it's tough to get them to eat when you want, so don't be afraid to pick up the bowl after 20 minutes and wait to try again until the next meal.

Don't free-feed Fifi. She has to learn to eat when her food is offered, not whenever she wants. If she really doesn't have an appetite, take her to the veterinarian.

There are a lot of recipes for raw and home-cooked diets for dogs, and some of those might be suitable for your dog, but you'll have to ask your veterinarian for advice and do some extensive

research. Simply feeding your dog willy-nilly can cause serious health problems, even imbalances that can lead to death. However, when done right, homemade diets are very healthful.

If Poochie is eating a good-quality balanced food, he doesn't need to eat a lot. For example, the average dog of about 15 pounds will eat only about $\frac{1}{2}$ cup of dry food and 2 tablespoons of wet food per day, split into two meals. This doesn't sound like a lot, but it's more than enough of good-quality food. You'll have to feed a lot more of the cheaper stuff to get the proper nutrition, which is part of the reason why it's not all that economical to try to save a few pennies on Poochie's diet. And remember, the more you feed, the more there is to pick up at walk time.

SUPPLEMENTS

It's not a bad idea to add a skin supplement, like an oil or powder, to your dog's food. Some people also add things like algae, nutritional yeast, glucosamine and other healthful supplements. Make sure that the supplement you add isn't going to imbalance your dog's system, as some vitamins and minerals can do. Offer the supplement only every other day or skip a few days between dosages. It's best to ask your veterinarian for advice before adding anything to your dog's diet.

FEEDING THE SENIOR DOG

Senior dogs need a senior-formula dog food and extra supplements to promote joint and skin health. Seniors can become plump, which can cause all sorts of health problems, including skeletal and respiratory issues. A dog is considered a "senior" when he's in the last third of his life expectancy. For example, if the average lifespan for the breed is 12 years and he's 8, then he's a senior, even if he's still spunky. Senior diets tend to be lower in calories and protein and higher in fiber, making it easier on the kidneys and digestive system. Even if your dog still acts like a pup as he enters his senior years, it's a good idea to be proactive with his changing dietary and health needs.

TREATS

Treats are essential for training and they show our dogs how much we love them (or at least that's the

perception). But too many treats can lead to a porky puppy, which leads to excessive veterinary bills. Keep treats to a minimum. Cut commercial treats in half or thirds, and offer veggies like carrots as healthful, low-cal snacks. A whole carrot makes a fun chew toy.

Primping the Pocket Pooch

I f you have a short-coated pocket pooch, you won't need to worry about finding a groomer, but many tiny dogs have long hair or are meant to be coiffed into a specific style, which requires a trip to the salon. No matter what breed you have, you do have to consider how to care for your dog's coat, skin, eyes, nails and teeth.

If Fluffy's name is not ironic (he's a Maltese, not an American Hairless), you'll need quite a few grooming tools to keep him from matting. In general, most dogs that need grooming go to a professional groomer. If you don't know what you're doing, it's possible to make Fluffy look less like a pampered pooch and more like he has a terrible skin condition. So don't bother buying clippers unless you plan on learning what to do with them.

DOING A DOGGIE-DO

Dog groomers don't have to be certified to do a doggie-do, like hairdressers for humans. So it's possible for anyone with clippers to call himself a dog groomer. There are grooming associations and societies that groomers can join, and it's a good sign if your potential groomer is a member, but that is not necessarily a testament to his background, education or experience.

The best way to find the right groomer is by word of mouth. Ask some of the dog owners in your neighborhood who they use, ask your veterinarian and call your local shelters to find out which salon has a great reputation. Some groomers work at large pet-supply shops, some work in small salons and some work at home. You can't judge a groomer by the size of his workplace. Some groomers have mobile salons and will come to you—it can't be more convenient.

Once you have been recommended to a particular groomer or salon, visit and watch how the dogs are treated. The staff should have a good rapport with the animals and good manners with the owners. Ask whether they know how to groom your particular breed. Some dogs, like the wire-coated breeds, may need to be "hand-stripped" rather than clippered, and not every groomer knows how to do this properly.

Ask how long the salon has been in business and what kind of experience the groomers have. Many conditions, such as tumors and skin problems, are easily identified by seasoned groomers, so it pays to have someone who has

been around the block a time or two. Also, ask if they regularly deal with small dogs. Often dogs are left under the dryers by themselves, and a small dog can easily become overheated.

How does the salon smell? Who's watching the pets while they are under the dryers? Is there a veterinarian that the salon uses in case of emergency? The salon should take extensive background information on your dog and require that he is up-to-date on his vaccinations.

CROOMINC SOCIALIZATION

Take your dog to the groomer as soon as he has had enough vaccinations to be able to be around other dogs (your veterinarian will let you know when). Even before then, you can visit the grooming salon with him (just don't put him down on the floor). Get him used to visiting the place and getting treats there. Ideally, he should look forward to going there so that it will not be a traumatic experience when you leave him there for the first time.

Before Yappers gets groomed for the first time, socialize him to all of the elements of grooming

that he's going to experience every two to four months for the rest of his life. Brush him gently to get him used to that sensation. Pick up his feet and gently rub each pad and touch each nail. Look into his ears and lift up his cheeks to expose his teeth. Hold his muzzle gently closed for three to five seconds. Show him a blow dryer and give him a treat when he approaches it. Then turn it on and blow the warm air onto him, treating and praising. Give him treats for good behavior and praise him. Make it a fun game that you play twice a day

for about ten minutes each time. When your veterinarian gives the green light, give him a short bath in warm water, making the experience as pleasant as possible.

SKIN CARE

As with humans, much of a dog's skin health has to do with how healthy he is inside, not just outside. You know that no cream, scrub or special formula can beat good nutrition, and the same holds true for your dog. You can give your pooch a supplement, such as Derm Caps, that will help to keep his skin healthy; also ask your vet about other supplements that are beneficial to the skin and can be added to the dog's food.

Don't be frugal about the shampoo that you use on your dog, because the inexpensive types can dry out his skin. Unhealthy dry skin means unhealthy dry hair. Why would you splurge on the good stuff for yourself and leave Scruffy with low-budget hair care? Dogs on the wrong diet can also get dandruff and a dry coat. You'd be amazed at the difference a good diet can make in terms of coat quality. Brushing also helps to keep the skin healthy, as it distributes oils throughout the coat and helps to loosen dandruff.

If you notice that your dog has a rotten odor on his skin, or you notice pustules or scabbing (oh, horror!), it's time for a visit to the veterinarian. Skin problems can be an indication of a fungus, bacteria, virus, parasite or hormonal imbalance.

GROOMING GEAR

For everyday (or few-times-a-week) grooming for a longhaired dog, you'll need a slicker brush, a pin brush and a wide-toothed comb. If your dog is sensitive, you can get a slicker brush for the sensitive areas. For a short-coated dog, you'll need a curry comb, bristle brush or grooming glove, and possibly a shedding blade. If your dog sheds a lot, get a hair magnet or other de-shedding tool. Your groomer can also give Furry a special shedding treatment that removes a lot of dead hair from the coat and also helps to reduce future shedding.

BATH TIME

Most dogs don't need to be bathed until they start smelling a little doggy or they get into something stinky outdoors. Once a month is probably a good rule, but some dogs only need to be bathed once every two or three months, or perhaps even just a few times a year. Your particular dog's breed and coat will determine how often he needs a b-a-t-h.

If you have a peanut-sized dog, you can bathe him in the kitchen sink. Fill the bottom up with warm water (not too hot, not too cool) and have him stand inside. Wet him thoroughly and then add shampoo to his body, avoiding his head. Don't ever get soap and water in his eyes and ears. To be safe, you can put a small drop of mineral oil into his eyes just before the bath. If your dog is a little larger, bathe him in the bathtub using a hose nozzle attachment (found in any pet shop or hardware store). When you're done, use a wet washcloth (water only) to wipe the dog's head and face. The "pug-faced" breeds will need special attention to the facial folds; these should be cleaned regularly, not just at bath time.

Beware of using flea shampoo on a little doggie because it may be too harsh for his small system. Instead, use a shampoo that has all-natural ingredients. If you have a white dog, you can find a special shampoo that removes stains and yellow coloring from white coats. There are shampoos for red- and yellow-colored dogs too. Don't use human shampoos on your dog because he needs a product with a different pH than you do; a human shampoo will dry out his skin more easily. If you have a longhaired dog, you might want to use a detangling conditioner or a spray-in detangler after rinsing out the shampoo.

Pat the wet pooch dry with a fluffy towel or a microfiber cloth; do not rub his coat or you risk creating tangles. If he's got a lot of coat, like a Pomeranian, you can blow-dry him on a warm setting as you brush his hair gently in the opposite direction of the way it grows. Don't let the dog get overheated.

SPA STUFF

Pocket poochies love being pampered (or it might be the owners who love doing the pampering, but we won't quibble

over the difference). Just about anything that you can find for yourself, you can find for Molly too. Aromatherapy, essential oils, nose and paw balms, flower essences, bath bars and more are among an endless array of products to make Molly smell like anything from freshly laundered linens to lavender or bubble gum.

THE NAIL SALON

Most people allow their groomers or vets to trim their dogs' nails, but it's fairly easy to learn how to do it yourself. If you choose to trim your dog's nails at home, get a guillotine-style nail trimmer made for cats or a notched nail scissor and make sure that you don't cut into the quick of the nail (the living part, which will bleed if cut). You can also gently file the nails once a week to keep them short.

If you want Princess to have the perfect poochie pedicure, try dog-specific nail *paw*lish. It dries quicker than regular polish, only needs one coat and is safe to use—you can even paint your nails to match. Now all you have

to do is get Princess to quit wriggling for a second so you can apply it.

BETTER TO HEAR YOU WITH

It's important to keep Taffy's ears clean, but you can't just go digging in there with a cotton swab. Don't ever stick anything in your dog's ears! When you clean the ears, use a moistened cotton ball; even then, you should clean only the areas that you can see (don't go tunneling into the dog's head). Use an ear-cleaning solution and/or a drying powder, especially with drop-eared dogs whose ear canals don't get a lot of airing out. Take Yippers to the vet if you smell a rotten odor in the ears or if you notice a sticky brown discharge or small dark specks.

BETTER TO SEE YOU WITH

Some dogs have excessive discharge from the eyes, which you can just wipe away daily with a moistened washcloth. Make sure not to scratch or irritate the dog's eyes. Some of the "bug-eyed" breeds can have dry eyes that require special drops or may have other eye problems that need to be monitored by a veterinarian.

THOSE PEARLY WHITES

Feed Rocky some dry kibble or hard biscuits daily; crunchy foods help to clean the plaque from his teeth as he chews. When you visit the vet, have your veterinarian check your dog's teeth to make sure that tartar isn't building up. The doctor might recommend a full dental cleaning, which requires anesthetic. Some dogs, like the brachycephalic breeds (short-muzzled breeds, like the Pug) and teacup dogs, don't fare well under anesthesia, so be sure to discuss this with your veterinarian.

GROOMING THE OLDER DOG

Older dogs get aches and pains just like older humans. They can become arthritic and can injure themselves more easily with daily activities. Most little dogs can live to be 15 years old or more, but they usually don't slow down until they're into their double digits. Nonetheless, make sure that your groomer understands your dog's limitations. As he gets older, your dog may not want his legs and paws to be touched in a certain way, and you and your groomer have to respect that. The dog can't tell you that he's hurting or stiff.

Keep up with your senior dog's grooming to keep him looking and feeling good. Pay attention to any changes in the coat and/or skin. Older dogs benefit from an extra-conditioning shampoo to bring out the luster in a drying coat.

AT THE BOTTOM OF THE POCKET

I hope you've enjoyed reading about pocket pooches and have learned something along the way. Here are ten things to remember, if you remember nothing else:

1. Pocket pooches aren't accessories, though you can get lots of cool accessories to go with them.
2. Fur is always sporty, so take your pocket pooch wherever you go.
3. Sure, you can't wear white after Labor Day, but you can make an exception for carrying around your Maltese, Coton, Bichon or Poodle.
4. Little black dogs are always flattering.
5. Clean-cut is always fashion forward—don't let your poochie get too scruffy.
6. Less is always more—have only as many pocket pooches as you have pockets.
7. Money can't buy you taste and it may not be able to buy you love, but it can buy you a great dog trainer (and perhaps even a cute one).
8. Don't match, coordinate. You don't have to get two of a kind to be cool.
9. Teacup dogs scream, "I'm a slave to fashion!" Go with the average size instead, unless you travel a lot or live in a studio apartment.
10. It's not always what's on the outside that counts. A peaceful inside is always chic, for both owner and doggie.

INDEX